MY DO, DIDDYMEN AND KNOTTY ASH POETRY

by

Michael Bartram

Grosvenor House
Publishing Limited

This book is published by
Grosvenor House Publishing Ltd
Link House
140 The Broadway, Tolworth, Surrey, KT6 7HT.
www.grosvenorhousepublishing.co.uk

A CIP record for this book
is available from the British Library

ISBN 978-1-80381-415-5

For my beautiful Diddy Granddaughters,
Alba and Nola x

Contents

The amazing artwork you will come across throughout this book was kindly provided by Allan Taylor, Gladys Chucklebutty, Daniel Hanton and Lee Joyce, a very talented group of Doddy fans!

Introduction

As many poems in this book will reveal, I have been a big fan of Sir Ken Dodd ever since I was a little boy. His humour, his stage presence, the Diddymen and the wonderful, magical world of Knotty Ash fascinated me.

Like most young children, I had a very vivid, active imagination and the thought of a very zany looking Doddy, his Diddymen and a land consisting of jam butty mines, treacle wells, broken biscuits, gravy trains, Moggy Ranch and a Black Pudding Plantation fired my imagination into overdrive!

I eventually moved to Knotty Ash and spent 15 lovely years there, living just a minute or so from Doddy's house. I was fortunate to bump into him several times; I have written about those lovely encounters in this book.

After Doddy sadly passed away, I compiled a tribute book called *Absent Friends…A Tribute To Sir Ken Dodd*. The book consisted of sincere, loving tributes from his fans, the media, colleagues from the entertainment world and others. My contributions were in the form of poetry. The book also included some amazing artwork sent in by his fans. Lady Dodd, gave the book her full approval and was its editor.

A few months after the book was published, I had collected enough material for a follow-up tribute book, but work on that book was delayed for a number of reasons, not least because the Coronavirus pandemic was reaching a peak.

On reflection, however, the balance of the new book was a little uneven, as it contained too much of my own poetry. Therefore, I decided to retain just a dozen or so of my poems and the rest I would publish as a separate publication... so that is how *this* book came to be!

I will continue to work on the compilation tribute book (*Remembering The One And Only Sir Ken Dodd*), which hopefully will be published in the autumn of 2024.

In the meantime, I hope you enjoy this collection of my own poetry dedicated to Doddy, his Diddymen and Knotty Ash, in which my *still* very active imagination played a great part!

Take care.

Michael Bartram 2023

Introductory Poem:
'The Map of Famous Knotty Ash'

Hello, there is *nothing* Diddy about this poem. It is 21 verses long and by far the longest poem in the book! 'The Map of Famous Knotty Ash' serves as an introduction to some of the unique and wonderful places in Knotty Ash you will come across in this book. Many of these places will of course be familiar to you, but lots of others are hidden gems. In your imagination they can be found too... as they were in *my* imagination, where I discovered them!

Happy exploring, everybody... Happy exploring!

The Map of Famous Knotty Ash

The map of Knotty Ash was given to me.
So many wonderful things on it to see.
A place where Airplanes *and* boats come.
A world of magic and a Diddy land of fun!

Knotty Ash is famous as Doddy's home.
And for many other things it's known.
Some of them may be a surprise to you.
Like the Knotty Ash harbour, what a view!

Knotty Ash Airport, bet that's a surprise!
Where Doddy Airlines take to the skies.
Only Diddy planes, that Diddy pilots fly.
But Diddy or not, they climb just as high!

On the map are the famous Treacle Wells.
Like hot cakes this sticky treacle sells.
Close by in the west, the Jam Butty Mines.
And to the east, the two Gravy Train lines.

Next to the TV studios on Diddy Parade.
A factory where repairs to biccies are made.
And if they can't be fixed, then that's OK.
For broken biscuits, just half price you pay!

On the map, the Moggy Ranch is in red.
The colour of Doddy's coat, it has to be said!
The Black Pudding Plantation, that's in black.
That area is a little bit off the beaten track.

Cont.

2

New on the map, a Knotty Ash gym to find.
An unusual gym, in fact it's *one* of a kind!
If your chuckle muscles have faded or gone.
Then visit this gym on the edge of Old Swan.

By Doddy's old school, on the map you'll see.
The Knotty Ash Bank, open each day till 3.
The Beach and Harbour, you can't miss them!
To go there, take the Doddy Bus, number 10!

On the map, heading towards Broadgreen.
Is home of the Doddy Knotty Ash footy team.
They lose every game, season after season.
Doddy being in goal is probably the reason!

The gentle folk of Knotty Ash, love a swim.
The baths are located next door to the gym.
A shallow pool, changing rooms are small.
Because all the swimmers are Diddy *not* tall!

Not on the map, as *just* the Diddymen know.
The landing site in Knotty Ash of a UFO!
Unsmiling Aliens, who landed on our Earth.
Then learnt to laugh for all they were worth!

The Doddy Museum, where visitors flock.
Is easy to find, next to the Knotty Ash clock.
A funny looking clock, it has a Doddy face!
The son of Knotty Ash, it can never replace.

If you like a jam butty with your afternoon tea.
The quaint Cafe Doddy is the place to be!
Going on foot or by car, Missus, it's easy to find.
It's by Springfield Park, which is clearly signed!

Cont.

The Doddy Arms pub, by the roundabout.
Sit yourself in The Snug, Missus, with a stout!
And to the north is the massive Great Hill
Close by is the lovely Squire Bar and Grill.

There's the barber shop that never shuts.
They don't do sensible, neat and tidy cuts.
They do zany Doddy haircuts, night and day.
It's *not* on the map, but it's next to Alder Hey.

Just past Dicky Mint Lane and to its right.
Is the Comedy University, so happy and bright!
And as unis go, it's not *all* that old or grand.
But it is the happiest university in the land!

On the map is the forever-busy Tourist Board.
Year after year, visiting figures have soared.
And on this Knotty Ash map, that is not all.
Hidden away is its very own Diddy Town Hall.

So, jump on the Doddy Bus, and go for a ride.
Visit the Knotty Ash Tourist Board for a guide.
Go to all those places on the map you can see.
Please say a big 'Hello' if you bump into me!

You'll find a cinema *and* a theatre to boot!
And Happiness Hall on the Doddy Bus route.
Don't forget Little Bongs, its name is unique!
And Doddy Towers, *I* moved in there last week!

The Happiness Train has a station of its own.
What better place could you ever call home?
Then in the south is famous Thomas Lane.
We have Doddy to thank for all this L14 fame!

So, with your Knotty Guidebook in your hand.
Visit the Knotty Ash FC or the Theatre Grand.
Study the map, you'll see there's plenty to do.
And you might even meet a Diddyman or two!

The Map of Famous Knotty Ash

1... The University of Comedy
2... The Doddy Arms Pub
3... The Knotty Ash Airport
4... The Chuckle Muscle Gym
5... The Jam Butty Mines
6... Dicky Mint Lane
7... The Treacle Wells
8... The beach & harbour
9... Doddy Towers
10... The Black Pudding Plantation
11...The Happiness Train Station
12... The Gravy Train Line
13... Sir Ken Dodd's home

14... The Happiness Hall
15... Knotty Ash Town Hall
16... The Doddy Bar & Grill
17... St John The Evangelist Church
18... The Doddy Cinema
19... Knotty Ash Doddy FC
20... The Broken Biscuit Repair Factory
21... The Knotty Ash Grand
22... Little Bongs
23... The Knotty Ash TV Studio
24... The Cafe Doddy
25... The Moggy Ranch
26... The Knotty Ash Tourist Board

The secret UFO landing site is not on the map – sorry (it is a Diddymen Top Secret!) However, you can read all about the landing and the Alien visit to Knotty Ash later on in the book!

CHAPTER 1

The Happiness Train Series of Poetry 1–10

'The Happiness Train' began life as a one-off poem, based on a special train service run solely for Doddy fans. The idea was that fans would board the train with payment just a big happy smile. Passengers would then travel to various Doddy-related locations of their choice, sharing happy Doddy stories, anecdotes and memories along the way.

The concept grew and grew and the Happiness Train became part-fantasy and imaginary in certain poems ('Dicky Mint the Train Driver', for example). In others I took a more realistic approach, based on the possible reality of such a train!

Spread out over two chapters, there are 20 Happiness Train poems in this book.

There are another eight poems in this series; those eight will be part of the future Doddy compilation tribute book I am hoping to publish in 2024.

All the passengers you come across on board the various trains are real Doddy fans. Either they are the lovely, dedicated followers of our hero, whom I have met in person, or are my friends on the fabulous Doddy Facebook groups.

I hope you enjoy reading this series of poems as much as I have enjoyed writing them!

The Happiness Train 1 (Introduction)

A train that runs on the special Doddy Line.
It leaves Lime Street soon from platform 9.
Anybody out there fancy an overnight ride.
One of the Diddymen might sit by your side!
I'll make some butties, if I can find the jam!
I'll bring broken bickies, especially for Sam!
Leave the house now, you'll catch this train.
Only a few tickets for the journey remain!
When I say 'tickets' do you know the score?
Well, you will if you've been on board before!
You don't need a ticket on device or in hand.
Not to travel on the happiest train in the land!
All you need to be is a Doddy fan with a smile!
To enjoy happiness and fun with every mile!

The Happiness Train 2 (A Local Route!)

I'm off to Broadgreen station, not too far.
It's only five minutes from Knotty Ash by car.
I have made jam butties, now in the boot.
For the Happiness Train, just a local route!

On board, many familiar happy faces I see.
Lulabelle Mac, Stephen Windle, and now me!
Our train won't be going too far up the track.
We're only off to the city centre and back!

We visit all the theatres Doddy has played.
All the memories they bring will never fade.
The Empire, Everyman, The Philharmonic Hall.
Non-stop laughter, from curtain raise to fall.

On The Royal Court wall, I see murals of Ken.
To Lime Street Station, we are all off to, then!
Into the statue of Doddy, our cameras zoom.
Then we visit Doddy's bust in the Picton Room.

It's been a lovely day, but now it's getting late.
The Happiness Train waits for us on platform 8.
The three princesses and Denise Potter their mum.
Go home after a day out of happiness and fun!

The Happiness Train 3 (The Wirral Line Trip!)

With a whistle and toot, and some Diddy steam.
The Happiness Train departs from platform 13.
Today it leaves Central Station on the Wirral Line.
Just a smile required to board, no ticket, no fine!

I wonder which Doddy fans are travelling today.
As we travel to the opposite side of Liverpool Bay.
Vera Yorke, Rosemarie Jones, no surprise there!
And I see Debs Fisher, Anne McAlan and Pat Adair!

We travel to New Brighton, the lovely Floral Hall.
I saw T. Rex perform there, a brilliant night I recall!
But later the theatre closed, in a dilapidated state.
But after a major facelift, opened its doors in 2008.

Doddy was the last to play there the previous year.
Then in December he was the first artiste to appear.
To christen the new stage, who better to choose?
Than the king of comedy, nobody will fill his shoes!

Not far to walk to our next New Brighton Location.
So, the Happiness Train we left at Atherton Station.
Ken reopened the book shop, there in 2016.
More lovely memories, what a happy day it's been!

Memories of the greatest comic we've ever known.
Pictures we shared on the Happiness Train home.
Irene Walsh was on board and I see Stephen Main.
As Dicky Mint takes us home on the Happiness Train

The Happiness Train 4 (On Tour!)

I've seen the Houses of Parliament and Big Ben.
The Happiness Train is at Euston, platform 10.
I went to Buckingham Palace to see the King.
Dicky Mint came with me on this day in spring!

Off to Blackpool next, for a walk along the prom.
For a mile those Christmas lights brilliantly shone.
But at the Theatre Grand, that was not so bright.
Since Doddy left us, it's lost its most shining light.

Dicky and I left Blackpool, Doddy's second home!
Next on the Happiness Train, we travelled to Frome.
A beautiful part of the world, Doddy took by storm!
At the Memorial Theatre, The Squire used to perform.

Frome is in Somerset, a lovely historic market town.
But now it was getting late, the sun was going down.
So as that sun was disappearing in the Somerset sky.
It was time for Dicky Mint and I to say 'Goodbye'

We headed back to Liverpool, our memories to share.
Other Doddy fans were on board, Dicky sat by Claire.
And on this Happiness Train, who better I have to say.
Than to have John Martin, telling jokes along the way!

The Happiness Train 5 (A Christmas Outing!)

With just a smile, bright and broad.
The Happiness Train, you can board.
An invitation to all you Doddy fans.
Make it part of your Christmas plans!

The Train departs on Christmas Eve.
From Lime Street Station it will leave.
Early morning start, from platform 3.
Make sure you're on this train with me!

Guaranteed joy and happiness galore.
Discover what chuckle muscles are for!
Dicky Mint and his mates will be there.
The sounds of laughter will fill the air!

We can share our Doddy jokes or tales.
Tears of laughter assured; it never fails!
Christmas lunch, and a glass of wine.
We'll toast the funniest man of all time!

A Doddy joke with every cracker we pull.
This train of Doddy fans is sure to be full!
Just twelve more sleeps, then away we go!
On the happiest train, you will ever know.

The Happiness Train 6 (The Funniest Man Ever... The Happiest Ever Train!)

Ever been on this special train before?
If not, jump aboard for happiness galore!
At the station, leave behind all your woes.
At 2pm today the Happiness Train goes!

It leaves from Lime Street, rain or shine.
No need to book a ticket, just be on time!
Just give a big smile and the journey is free!
And Dicky Mint will greet you on platform 3.

Other Diddymen too will be coming along.
You'll hear them sing their Diddymen song!
Lunch served off a menu from Knotty Ash.
So, gravy from the gravy trains on your mash!

Help yourself to broken biscuits from a box!
Jam butties fresh from Knotty Ash stocks.
But all mines and factories are closed today.
Because for the Diddymen it's a day of play!

And so no Moggy skins from the ranch to sell.
And no treacle today pulled up from the well.
Come on Doddy fans, join in the fun and cheer.
Come onboard for the first journey of this year!

Bring along your tickling stick, wave it in the air.
Pull some funny faces and ruffle up your hair!
Let's have a laugh together all in Doddy's name.
The funniest man ever... the happiest ever train

The Happiness Train 7
(We Are Having a Ball!)

A rainbow of colour, puffs of happy smoke.
A train full of passengers of like-minded folk!
A lovely blue sky overhead the Doddy Line.
Dicky Mint the driver, having left platform 9.
As the Happiness Train rolls down the rails.
Doddy fans share their memories and tales.
The buffet car is open for a jam butty treat.
As well as a choice of broken biscuits to eat!
You don't need a ticket of course for this ride.
Instead, just give a big smile, happy and wide!
Blackpool North is the train's next port of call.
Join Linda and Sandra, we're having a ball!
I wouldn't expect *anything* less on *this* Train.
Just like *everything* else in our Doddy's name!

The Happiness Train 8
(Vera Yorke and the Thomas Lane Dash!)

Puffs of happiness smoke can be seen.
At the station in Liverpool's Broadgreen.
As just pulling in, is the Happiness Train.
Vera alights and runs down Thomas Lane.

Other big Doddy fans quickly follow suit.
To Knotty Ash, they are now all on route.
Just what's the attraction, I hear you say?
Why all this happiness and joy on display?

Because Thomas Lane, is a magical place.
It's the home of Doddy... his one life base.
And Vera will see many a Jam Butty Mine.
As she fast approaches a Knotty Ash sign!

And Treacle Wells will also be in her view.
As Knotty Ash has got many of them too!
But most of all it's got Doddy... the Squire.
What else in the world, could it ever require?

The Happiness Train 9
(The Buffet Menu)

Only a small buffet selection, I'm afraid.
We do have jam butties, freshly made!
Being very scrumptious, from the mine.
Those butties sell out most of the time!

And broken biscuits, we have them too.
And 'gottles of geer'... Knotty Ash brew!
If you like treacle, we have that to sell.
It's from Knotty Ash, *that* famous well!

The menu is hardly a proper menu at all.
But still on this train, you can have a ball!
Yes, it's *only* a Diddy buffet, on this ride.
But lots of happiness... we still provide!

Happiness Train 10... The Delay!

A Platform announcement for all Doddy fans.
'We are sorry for this Diddy delay to your plans.
Your Happiness Train driver has been taken ill.
He strained his chuckle muscles while in Rhyl!

'It was against our best advice we have to say.
But the driver listened to Doddy jokes on the way!
His sides soon split with laughter; ribs were sore.
But the driver continued to listen to some more!

'By the time the hysterical driver got to platform 6.
He was out of control and seen waving tickling sticks!
He was taken to a Diddy hospital and is doing well.
All his visitors are warned... *no* Doddy jokes to tell!

'As we can't risk a relapse, while he's on the mend.
So just your best wishes, we think it's best to send.
And for all you big Doddy fans Knotty Ash-bound.
A replacement Happiness Train driver we've found!

'*But* we have a sneaky feeling; he's a Doddy fan too!
But we *have* to get the Happiness Train to you!
So, from all Doddy jokes, he *has* to agree to refrain.
Then *his* chuckle muscles, he won't also pull or strain!'

The Happiness Train (with a new driver!) continues its
adventures in Chapter 7 with a further 10 poems... Until then,
toot toot!

CHAPTER 2

Poetry (Including Fans' Artwork)

Fingers Crossed!

I filled in a job application form today.
There's a vacancy down Knotty Ash way.
To help in the wells and Jam Butty Mines.
As Dicky Mint says, these are busy times.

Paid in jam butties, it's easier that way.
As on jam butties, there is no tax to pay!
They are taking people over Diddy height.
To work, happy Diddy shifts, day or night!

They teach you how to drive a gravy train.
To fix broken biscuits, chocky and plain.
On the Moggy Ranch, they need a hand.
As it's the only such ranch across the land!

I think as a child, from the age of two or three,
A Diddyman, I told my Mum, I wanted to be.
But as a child, I grew up very fast and tall.
So not much chance for me, not much at all!

To be close friends with Dicky Mint and co.
And to perform with Ken Dodd on every show.
They were the sort of things I wanted to do.
Alas my dream was not destined to come true!

Cont.

Now later in my life, a new chance has come.
To be a Diddyman of sorts, and join the fun.
My form filled in, so keep fingers crossed for me.
The oldest, tallest Diddyman you'll ever see!

Diddy Tears

The Moggy Ranch was closed today.
And Knotty Ash jam in the mines did stay.
The gravy trains did not take to the track.
No repaired biscuits in the factory to pack.
Snuff quarries where so quiet, not a sound.
All over Knotty Ash, no Diddymen around.
Today the Diddymen had no treacle to sell.
As Diddymen tears had filled up the well.
In those wells, I saw a million tears so small.
Just room for one more... so I let mine fall.

The Table Is Set!

You are invited to Knotty Ash for a snack.
Pull up a Diddy chair, relax and sit back.
'What a beautiful day' so tuck in and eat.
And today, the Diddymen you can meet!
Please have a jam butty while you're here.
Our jam is lovely, this time of the year!
Sample the Treacle, it's fresh from the Well.
More scrumptious than the shops will sell!
How do you prefer your gravy, thick or thin?
Hot off the Gravy Train, that's just come in.
Dip a broken biscuit into your cup of tea.
It couldn't be fixed in the factory you see!
So, for my Doddy friends, the table is set.
For Gladys, Kathleen and young man Brett!

Be Prepared!

Be prepared for a night of laughs galore!
The legendary Doddy's on a Happiness Tour!
Liverpool's Royal Court, Blackpool's Grand.
Beautiful theatres, up and down the land!

Shanklin Theatre, Victoria Hall, Stoke On Trent.
Four or even five hours on stage will be spent!
Yet our Doddy's no spring chicken anymore.
But the 'Sold Out' signs will be up for sure!

What a trooper Ken Dodd is at such an age.
To still give so much of his life to the stage.
Such amazing devotion, dedication and drive.
To still be touring the country, performing live!

Still putting our 'chuckle muscles' to the test.
Still the 'master of mirth' and the 'king of jest'
So, get your Doddy ticket now, join the queue.
But don't expect to get home until well after 2!

The Great Hill of Knotty Ash

Next to the University of Comedy it's by.
Hardly the biggest hill, and that's no lie!
But to a Diddyman, it's of massive height!
A challenge to conquer it, day or night!
Dicky Mint tried it once, but had to stop.
But he did get very close to the top!
He showed great courage and huge will.
To reach the summit of Knotty Ash Hill!
University students often meet at its base.
Especially if the sun is wearing a smiley face!
The students chill out there on their break.
Before their next comedy lesson to take!
On the Knotty Ash landscape, it's the peak.
Another lovely location in Knotty Ash to seek!

Doddy Park Opening Day Liverpool 14

Welcome to Doddy Park Opening Day.
There's no other park like it, I have to say!
It's a Happiness Park, it's one of a kind.
A similar park anywhere, you'll never find!

A park for Diddymen and for people tall.
Doddy Park in Knotty Ash, a park for all!
A park where children can play carefree.
Under a rainbow of light, for us all to see.

Doddy Park is dog friendly, bring them too.
It's a beautiful park, with its beautiful view!
Visit its cafe, serving snacks hot and cold.
Broken biscuits and jam butties to be sold!

In the middle of Doddy Park, a musical treat.
It'll be a special place for Doddy fans to meet.
Because that is where the bandstand sits.
And every day you can hear big Ken Dodd hits!

The park has gardens, with flowers in bloom.
And for a Diddy Lake, they found the room!
Paddle if you wish, or a boat you can hire.
Doddy Park, a park dedicated to 'The Squire'

Cont.

For the children, there are swings and slides.
And a miniature Happiness Train, giving rides!
So, follow the 'Rainbow' signs, I'll see you there.
And a beautiful time together, we can share!

So, with her Doddy scissors, Irene cuts the bow.
And then into Doddy Park, all the visitors flow.
Colin, Denise and Lulabelle, among the first in.
A wonderful, happy day for all, is about to begin!

Brilliant artwork by the very talented Allan Taylor!

The Perfect Pro

Doddy paces in the wings awaiting his cue.
In his head a thousand jokes, old and new.
A spotlight splits the darkness with its beam.
Then the show starts, 'Happiness' its theme!

The familiar tune plays of which we never tire.
Then on stage walks the Knotty Ash Squire.
An all-out assault on the chuckle muscle begins
Flashlights bounce off red moggy coat skins.

On getting the last bus home, best not to bank.
More likely you'll be queuing in the taxi rank!
An understatement to say you'll get home late.
But you might hear milk rattling in its crate!

Jokes delivered from a canon, lightening quick.
Into the audience, thrown another tickling stick!
Doddy as ever on top form, from the word go.
Taking comedy to a new level... the perfect pro!

Knotty Ash Doddy FC

The worst footy team ever has to be.
The very bad Knotty Ash Doddy FC!
They play for laughs; they play for fun.
Not a single game have they ever won!

Doddy in goal, Dicky Mint at the back.
And the rest of the Diddymen in attack.
Every game, they concede at least 10.
They never score a goal, not even a pen!

Not a single ball, Doddy's ever caught.
And the team overall is a little bit short!
The funniest team ever, I have to say.
That's why we love to watch them play!

To a cup final, this team will never go.
A medal to their children, never to show!
But their games are shown live on TV.
On the Comedy Channel, for all to see!

John Brealey met Doddy one Friday in 1992 when travelling by train from Liverpool to his home in Wiltshire. His blog of that memorable meeting was published in *The Oldie Magazine* (21 November 2022).

Here is my brief poem telling of John's unforgettable encounter with the one and only Sir Ken Dodd!

One Man, One Train, Two Butties!

Like wave after wave, the jokes would flow.
As the legend Doddy gave a one-man show.
A one-man audience, a passenger on a train.
A tsunami delivery that nature couldn't tame!
The charisma of Doddy was second to none.
Where have the people like our Doddy gone?
Doddy wouldn't sit on a train and hide away.
As Doddy was a 'people's man' plain as day.
A stage to Doddy wasn't just a theatre or TV.
He made people chuckle wherever he may be.
Over two lopsided big butties, stuffed with jam.
Doddy put on a show, for one very lucky man!
What a journey that must have been for John.
It proves our Doddy is unique... the number one!

Sing a Song

Tonight, in Heaven, Doddy has a show planned.
An Easter Special concert in the Promised Land.
Songs of faith and prayer, the theme of the show.
Just like the choir boy Doddy of many years ago.

Backed by the angels from God's heavenly choir.
Will be the one and only... the Knotty Ash Squire.
Doddy will keep all the jokes under wraps tonight.
It's not that kind of show, no tickling stick in sight!

No Knotty Ash drum, no moggy skin coat to wear.
Doddy will look all dapper, he'll *even* tidy his hair!
Happy Easter, Doddy, we still miss and love you so.
Sing a song for us tonight, your absent friends below.

Doddy Talks to My Mum!

I stopped to get fuel in Tesco, Queens Drive.
When I bumped into the funniest man alive!
It so made my day, I couldn't believe my luck!
I tried to keep composed, not act starstruck

Customers in the shop, did whisper and stare.
A legend was among us, and I was there!
My hero, a comic genius, stood in the queue.
It was our Doddy of course, what should I do?

So, I paid for my petrol, then I waited outside.
Like a kid, my excitement I was unable to hide!
Clutching my packet of crisps and choccy bar.
I patiently waited for Doddy to return to his car.

Then when Doddy left the shop, I shouted 'Hi!'
He looked so dapper, in long coat, hat and tie.
Then to my surprise, Doddy walked over to me.
What an amazing day that turned out to be!

Doddy said 'Hello, hope you are well, young man.'
Then he made me laugh, like only Doddy can!
I politely asked The Squire, before he went home.
Could he say a brief 'Hi' to my mum on the phone?

Without pause, Doddy said that would be fine.
And of course, he stayed much longer on the line!
I thanked Doddy so much, he had made our day.
He wished me well, safe journey, then drove away.

**Sir Ken Dodd made my mum so happy on this occasion, when
he kindly made a surprise phone call to her... God bless them
both xx.**

The Best Medicine!

If you feel peaky and a Diddy bit frail.
You've tried medication, but to no avail.
A dose of our Doddy will do the trick.
It's worked for me, when I've felt sick!

So, the quickest way over colds and flu.
Is to simply watch a Ken Dodd Revue!
Laughter is the best medicine you see.
The cheapest cure... as laughter is free!

If you're under the weather, low in mood.
Then twice a day, to be taken with food.
Well, when I say 'food' a jam butty will do.
Watch a Doddy show, all the way through!

If you feel a little queasy... a tummy ache.
Then laughter is the best medicine to take!
Or maybe like me, your knee is very sore.
Listen to Doddy, he's by far the best cure!

Release those endorphins from your brain.
By taking a ride on the Happiness Train!
Or watch 'An Audience With'... better still!
I guarantee you, Missus, you'll no longer feel ill!

The Tickling Stick!

Doddy made them famous as we know.
They were part and parcel of each show.
Ticking sticks and Doddy...never apart.
He made them into a funny work of art!

But for what else can they be used for?
You *can* tickle with them, that's for sure!
Also can be used to conduct a brass band.
Or waving Diddy planes in to safely land!

On the Knotty Ash Town Hall roof, I see 2.
These in the colours of red, white and blue.
Knotty Ash magicians, for their every trick.
Don't wave a wand, they use a *tickling stick!*

Doddy's On Tour!

Doddy's on Tour, yes you heard right!
He's appearing up in Heaven tonight.
And this is not a special one-off show.
A heavenly tour, Doddy will undergo!

To see Doddy, there's such a demand.
So lots of shows, Doddy has planned.
I can picture the fun, the laughs galore.
Angels going home in the morning at 4!

An audience of all ages, sure to attend.
Comedy and songs our Doddy to blend.
From every cloud, will fall joyous tears.
So tonight, will be the wettest for years!

As promised, the first of three tales about the Knotty Ash UFO landing. Don't worry, Missus, they are very friendly Aliens!

UFO Over Knotty Ash!

A UFO hovered over Knotty Ash one day.
It came to study Earthlings at work and play.
It became invisible, it didn't make the news.
It landed in silence near Knotty Ash Mews.

From a distant world were nobody laughed.
The Aliens, one by one then left their craft.
The Aliens took to human form as planned.
And began their study of this faraway land.

They came across the Diddymen having fun.
They heard raucous laughter... tears to run!
They were puzzled by this unusual sound.
Using X-ray eyes, chuckle muscles they found!

Dicky Mint offered them a jam butty to eat.
Never had they tasted such a delicious treat!
The Aliens found themselves on Thomas Lane.
They came across a human, Doddy his name!

Cont.

His appearance came as a bit of a shock.
Was he typical, they thought, of human stock?
They approached Doddy, his tongue they spoke.
Doddy typically replied with a laugh and a joke!

Slowly but surely all the Aliens began to smile.
Then they fell about laughing and did for a while!
And so, it went on as they travelled about more.
Laughter and happiness was all the Aliens saw!

The Aliens before long, came to love this place.
And so, they never took off their human face.
Soon they had chuckle muscles of their very own.
And those Aliens to this day, never went home!

There are two follow-up poems about our friendly Knotty Ash visitors later in the book!

My Diary

A little look at my new diary of late.
Something missing from many a date.
Nothing written in pencil or in pen.
No Doddy events with his Diddymen.
That's something hard to get used to.
Not seeing when the next show is due.
Summer, winter, spring and the fall.
No 'Happiness Show' to mention at all.
No counting down to shows day by day.
It's sad to see my diary look this way.

To Knotty Ash

I just woke up to the sound of the bell.
A good night's sleep, a nice story to tell.
To Knotty Ash overnight I have been.
So this is what happened in my dream!
Sunshine, under suburban skies of blue.
I saw treacle on tap, so sticky like glue.
There was Dicky Mint and all his chums.
There was gravy trains on daily runs.
To be in such a place, how happy I am.
As I see some Diddymen mining for jam.
Then I saw them all again, having a treat.
Broken biscuits from the factory to eat!
To those Snuff quarries I was also shown.
A Moggy Skin coat, I was given to own!
The Diddymen sang their famous song.
A fantastic dream, what a place to belong!

**Another one of my Diddymen and Knotty Ash dreams....
I have them all the time, long may they continue!**

I Walked On Air!

A light went out on Thomas Lane.
But the happy memories still remain.
It's an impossible thing to replace.
The joy of laughter on Doddy's face!

Today on Thomas Lane, I had a walk.
Where Doddy and I often had a talk.
Only a few Diddy words to share.
But as I walked away, I walked on air!

As Doddy made people feel that way.
One chance meeting… one special day!
On Thomas Lane now, it's not the same.
But those memories, will always remain.

Thank you to Daniel Hanton for this superb artwork.

The Broken Biscuit Repair Factory Tour

In Knotty Ash, it's a special day.
So, to Liverpool 14, make your way!
Get there early and join the queue.
As a brilliant day is in store for you!

It is a one-off occasion... entry free.
The only place today you need to be!
Today they'll be opening their doors.
For three Broken Biscuit Factory tours!

Biscuits in pieces come to this place.
Broken in two or three, whatever the case.
They'll be soon repaired, fit to eat.
To dip in your cuppa, a morning treat!

On a conveyor belt, biscuits pass by.
And like a flash, in the blink of an eye!
The biccies are repaired, how is it done?
Find out on the tour and join in the fun!

Sorry Jon and Bugs!

This photograph was taken in about '71.
When I shared a room with my brother, Jon.
Jon is *very* talented, I'll let you know!
I've seen him on stage steal many a show!

Tucked up in bed, there's also Bugs Bunny.
A favourite character of mine, oh so funny!
So, with both lovely cartoon and family ties.
I have in store, a bit of a shock and surprise!

Sorry Jon and Bugs, you're the best by far.
But on this photo, the wallpaper is the star!
Nothing personal, little bruv, hope you agree.
But that wallpaper just means *so* much to me!

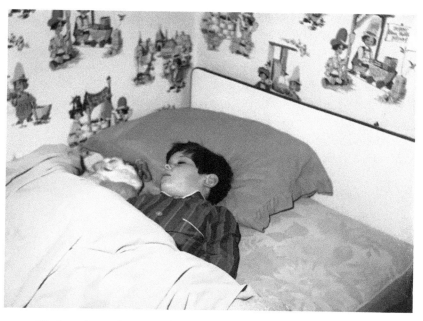

My lovely and very talented little brother in a rare pose
(he's not talking!). Just kidding, Bruv, luv ya loads!
Photo taken by my mum, Lil Bartram.

Behind The Mask

I look at a face hidden by a mask.
Who could it be, you may well ask!
So little to see behind the disguise.
But I do see laughter in those eyes!
I can't make out the mouth or chin.
I can't see if the face, is full or thin?
But I do see a mountain of crazy hair.
Could that be Doddy standing there?
If only he could utter a word or two.
As that would give me sufficient clue.
Then I realise, no need to speak.
It must be Doddy, as he is so unique!

**The second fantastic contribution for the
book, kindly provided by Allan Taylor**

Sir Ken Dodd MP (Mirth Politician!)

Westminster has a brand-new MP.
Sir Ken Dodd of Knotty Ash, OBE!
His election campaign was unique.
He just told funny jokes for a week!

His slogan was 'Happiness For All'.
That became Doddy's rallying call!
In Happiness Hall, came voting day.
Loads of Doddy rosettes on display!

Then the counting of votes begun.
Doddy got the lot, so he easily won!
Minister For Happiness, his new role.
Laughter Laws... Doddy to control!

Every town to get a happiness gym.
To keep our chuckle muscles in trim!
On best Doddy gags, MPs to debate.
MPs not allowed home until it's late!

Tickling Sticks waved to cast a vote.
The PM must wear a Moggy Skin coat!
Sir Ken Dodd MP, has set out his stall.
The nation will see 'Happiness For All'

My Doddy Dream

Doddy was in Heaven, this was my dream.
Making everyone laugh, tears to stream.
Angels and Saints all gathered around.
All over Heaven, one big laughing sound!
People at the gates, rushed to come in.
'Hurry up', said Doddy, with a toothy grin.
'Missus, this is free, put your purse away.'
'Bet you didn't think you'd see me today!'
Those without seats, sat upon a cloud.
No dogs, no show, so dogs were allowed!
A Doddy act might end late, oh so true!
So, St Peter had this plan of what to do.
Just in case his show finished far too late.
He gave Doddy the keys to Heaven's gate!

A Happy Heavenly 94th Birthday, 8 November 2021

A Birthday wish to Doddy, now a Heavenly 94.
The memories he left us, will last for evermore.
The joyous tears of laughter, we'll forever shed.
The funniest comedian ever, it has to be said!

And what about that voice, beautiful, every note!
A very funny looking man in his moggy skin coat!
The *best* ventriloquist ever…? OK, maybe not so!
But certainly, the funniest, that we'll ever know!

Value for money? Well, Doddy was out on his own.
Fans often saw the milkman, on their way home!
Such fantastic times, stored in our memory bank.
For all those great days, the birthday boy we thank.

'The Watch Tapper'
(In the Wings!)

Young man in the wings, leave your watch alone.
It's only midnight, much too early to go home!
He's tapping his timepiece, with glare in his eye.
I've only been on four hours, so I don't know why!
This full house is enjoying my Happiness Show.
And there's probably at least another hour to go!
A little bit later, Dicky Mint has to join me still.
I'll pay all of the overtime... just send me the bill!
I like to give Val and Phyllis value for money, you see.
And Pamela has come a long way, just to see me!
My late shows are legendary, tonight is not unique.
In fact, they have happened every night this week!
For now young man, have a jam butty or a Diddy nap
I'm carrying on, *even* if your watch, you tap, tap, tap!

For the Benefit of Doddy Fans

For the benefit of Doddy fans, tonight there's a show.
The sell-out crowd will wildly cheer as the lights go low.
Sir Ken will perform this evening until the hour is late.
So have your butty boxes ready and cancel your taxi date!

Doddy plays the Blackpool Grand by the sand and the sea.
It's one of Doddy's favourites, in Blackpool he loves to be!
All the Doddy fans will be there, the regulars and the new.
Vera, Jan, Sandra and Rosemarie Jones just to name a few!

Dicky Mint will come on stage and do the best he can.
But doubtless he'll upset Doddy if things don't go to plan!
Doddy will tell countless jokes, one after one he will fire.
He'll beat a drum upon the stage, in his moggy coat attire!

Sir Ken's beautiful voice will sing those hits of yesteryear.
Numbers that will bring you happiness and also leave a tear.
For the benefit of all Doddy fans, Sir Ken will again give his all.
The greatest artiste to adorn every theatre, pavilion or hall.

The Knotty Ash Times Newspaper

A new Knotty Ash newspaper launched today.
The 'Knotty Ash Times' is coming your way!
Only all the happy news, this paper will report.
All the local happiness and all the local sport!

If Doddy FC ever win, then we'll let you know.
But with Doddy in the goal, we don't think so!
The Happiness Train timetable will be on page 3.
And every day a special Doddy pull-out for free!

Every weekend edition comes with TV Guide.
Please note the Doddy TV shows on every side!
So, order a copy today, Missus, it'll sell out for sure.
And the Diddymen will deliver it right to your door!

The Happiness Light

Stars come and go, shine bright for a while.
They blow with the wind, in vogue or style.
Not too many entertainers can last the pace.
It takes somebody special to stay in the race.

Not too many can cross divides, bridge a gap.
To tour the circuit for decades, lap after lap.
But our Doddy did all that, you can't deny!
A one-off master of his craft, the reason why.

Now the master has left us, a huge gap to fill.
A mountain to climb, I doubt if anyone will.
Doddy fans sadly bid farewell just a year ago.
But the Happiness Light he left will forever glow.

Dicky Mint's Campaign!

I spoke to Dicky Mint on Dicky Mint Lane
He told me all about his Diddy campaign.
He wants a new public holiday to create.
To make Doddy's birthday a special date!
So he's wrote to the King and Number 10.
And explained his idea to the current PM!
Make the 8th of November a day of fun.
A day of happiness… no work to be done!
Street parties to be held across the land.
Unsmiling faces on that day to be banned!
Jam butties… the national dish of the day.
Funny Doddy language and words to say!
'What a beautiful day, Missus,' that day will be.
A country of happy, smiley faces to see!
Tickling sticks to be on display everywhere.
A day when happiness would fill the air!
The campaign has support from one and all.
So, the 'powers that be'… it's now your call!

Without Doddy

This early morning, I stood on Blackpool Prom.
Stood watching the people go by, one by one.
To my left slowly turned the Blackpool Wheel.
But something is missing from Blackpool, I feel.

In my shadow stood the Tower, proud and tall.
I heard the laughter of children and seagull's call.
I saw Doddy's name engraved on marble stone.
In a town some thought to be his second home.

Kicking the wet sand from beneath my feet.
I visited the Grand Theatre in a nearby street.
Doddy performed there often, well into the night!
A beautiful theatre, almost hidden out of sight.

Beneath the late summer sky, all clear and blue.
It was then time to go home, my train was due.
I still love magical Blackpool, and I always will.
But without our Doddy, it's got a huge hole to fill.

The Day Will Come

It's 2 o'clock in the morning, soon 3 then 4!
It's a cold, cold night and the rain does pour.
I'm not as young as I was, but a job to be done.
As I pack away the famous Knotty Ash drum.

The moggy skin coat I lay across the back seat.
Dicky Mint sits quietly, another show complete.
These times can be hard, but please hear this.
The day will come when these times I will miss.

Costumes, hats, tickling sticks all packed away.
Soon home to Knotty Ash, it's been a long day.
Doddy says his goodbyes, programmes to sign.
The bright theatre lights, they no longer shine.

One day I will sorely miss our after-show routine.
For year after year, we've made the perfect team!
We finally drive away, to make the journey home.
I will yearn for these times, when I am left alone.

Doddy Towers L14

I've just moved in to a new apartment block.
It's called 'Doddy Towers'... that's no shock!
I'm on the top floor, it's so beautiful up there.
With its magnificent view, beyond compare!

And there's something else you should know.
Though so high up, I can hear laughter below!
As Knotty Ash is so full of happiness and glee.
It's all those chuckle muscles working you see!

On this sunny day, with no clouds in the way.
I can see every Doddy landmark as clear as day.
From Dicky Mint Lane to the Happiness Hall.
From the harbour to the uni, I can see them all.

I can see Treacle Wells and Jam Butty Mines.
I can see a thousand 'Happy Doddy' tourist signs!
What a marvellous, unique and lovely scene.
I get from Doddy Towers, up on floor fourteen!

My Very Diddy Job!

I'm a Diddyman, Dicky Mint my name.
I go to work now on the Happiness Train.
On board I sing the 'Happiness Song'.
All the other passages soon sing along.

Today, treacle from the wells I will lift.
I only work for one hour, a Diddy shift!
Then to Knotty Ash station, platform 5.
And wait for the Happiness Train to arrive!

What's in today's lunch box, let me see.
Jam butties of course and a flask of tea.
And a tasty treacle pudding I'll also make.
I'll eat that for desert while on my break!

I get a thirty-minute break to eat and play.
'What a fantastic job that is,' I hear you say!
I'm a very lucky Diddyman, we all agree.
I finish my day's work at 4, and start at 3!

The Comedy University of Knotty Ash

Cambridge and Oxford University, it is not!
But one massive advantage this Uni has got.
It has one Professor Doddy, teaching his art.
That's what sets Knotty Ash University apart!

So, if a stand-up comedian you want to be.
And in that subject, you want to earn a degree.
Then by what better man could you be taught!
Than 'The King of Comedy'... one of a sort!

He'll teach you all of his craft, all of his tricks.
How to make the most of a pair of tickling sticks!
With witty assistant John Martin by his side.
You can attend this Uni with honour and pride!

And on graduation day, in cathedral of choice.
In having a degree in comedy, you can rejoice.
In moggy skin gown, throw your caps in the air.
Then be sure to fix your crown of sticky-up hair!

Jigsaw

I empty all the jigsaw pieces on to a tray.
I dig out the corners, then I'm on my way.
To the picture on the box, I constantly refer.
I find the edges to make the puzzle square.

I see what looks like part of a tickling stick.
It interlocks with a satisfying little click!
A puzzling piece I look at this way and that.
Until I realise it's part of Dicky Mint's hat!

I make out part of a butty, jam it contains.
A jagged segment, part of the gravy trains.
Coming together at last the Knotty Ash drum.
Soon my special jigsaw at last will be done.

Then finally, the last few pieces I easily find.
This Ken Dodd jigsaw was all in my mind.
Every piece I imagined was vital in some way.
To help make Doddy the legend, he is today.

Local Produce Aisle
(Knotty Ash Sainsbury's)

I went to shop in Sainsbury's with my list.
Boxes to tick, in case items I've missed!
I met Doddy a few years ago in this store.
We chatted away for a few minutes or more.

I was with my girls, when they were small.
He made them laugh, and so polite and all.
Two new young fans, Doddy made the day.
This is the Knotty Ash store, I meant to say!

And now I buy jam for my butties and pies.
Local produce of course, so it's no surprise!
That it's the very best jam, you'll ever taste.
Not one Diddy bit in my jar will go to waste!

Then I got treacle, which I love to eat neat.
Or I'll make pudding with it, for a lovely treat!
Next on my list, Knotty Ash gravy in aisle 3.
I need that later, when I go home for my tea.

Black puddings I bought for my brekky plate.
A full English breakfast every morning at 8!
My basket now full, today that's all I need.
One final item... a Doddy poetry book to read!

Easter Holiday TV

Easter holiday TV, I look at the guide.
Usual old stuff on each terrestrial side.
Two Bond films with Connery or Moore.
Nothing too exciting I haven't seen before.

Snooker's OK, I'll watch the odd frame.
Match of the Day, but *no* Liverpool game!
What we need is a special Easter treat.
Something brand new and not a repeat.

A telly programme from a bygone age.
With someone like Doddy up on the stage.
A TV audience of millions guaranteed!
A Doddy 'Easter Special' is what we need!

Full of laughter, songs, and Diddymen too.
No channel hopping as we usually do!
Just a nation watching Doddy on their TV.
If only this weekend we had that to see!

Nothing Can Compare!

The curtain is drawn and the stage is lit.
The audience is played an old Doddy hit.
On stage is the Great Knotty Ash drum.
A sell-out crowd await an evening of fun!
The excitement, you can feel in the air.
To such live shows nothing can compare!
Chuckle muscles, all ready to be strained.
This feeling over the years has never waned.
Then like a hurricane appears the great man!
To entertain us, like only The Squire can!
Fasten your safety belts for one heck of a ride.
Be ready to be filled full of happiness inside!
Plans to catch the last bus we can postpone.
Because it'll be long gone when we go home!

Little Bongs

Little Bongs, Knotty Ash, East Prescot Road.
A beautiful little spot, with an L14 postcode.
People ask, 'Is there really such an address?'
The simple answer being, most definitely yes!

Each day, when the sun rises in Little Bongs.
Listen very carefully... you'll hear some songs!
Because behind the cottages, sixteen in a row.
That's the way to work, the Diddymen will go!

Whether off to the mines, jam butties to make.
Or to a Treacle Well, the same route they take!
Singing 'We are the Diddymen' along their way.
The folk of Little Bongs, wave to them each day.

And the children of Little Bongs, sing along too.
They pretend to members of this working crew!
By Jove, Missus, wouldn't you love to live there?
As with lovely Little Bongs... nothing can compare!

To Create Magic

Making everyday things funny… that's a feat.
Like looking for a shirt or a jam butty to eat!
Gags about pants, older men shouldn't wear!
Making us laugh with his crazy style of hair!
Turning a feather duster into a tickling stick.
To create magic, without the need of a trick.
To transport us all to Knotty Ash and beyond.
To create an illusion, without wave of a wand.
Doddy could coax laughs from the mundane.
No other comic could quite do that the same!
But Doddy was 'no other comic', we all agree.
He saw a humour in things, only he could see.
He opened our eyes, his funny world he shared.
To Doddy in my life, no-one has ever compared.

The Landmark Clock of Knotty Ash

So, this clock can be seen by all.
As Knotty Ash goes, it's pretty tall!
A lovely landmark in the south.
Not far from the harbour mouth.
Special days, the clock will chime.
Doddy's birthday was the last time!
The Doddy clockface, quietly ticks.
On the roof are two huge tickling sticks.
These two sticks have a role to play.
Protecting Knotty Ash night and day.
Bit like Bertie and Bella I suppose.
Keeping at bay unwanted foes!
They keep Knotty Ash a happy land.
Just like Doddy had always planned!

Bertie and *Bella* are the 2 Liver Birds on top of the Liver Buildings watching over and protecting Liverpool!

Sir Ken Dodd and Sir Roger Hunt

Doddy ran onto the pitch, hair bolt upright.
Sticking his teeth out, in kit of red and white
He left the tunnel, touching the Anfield sign.
He just ate five jam butties during the half time!

Bill Shankly had a plan, to play Doddy upfront.
To pair him with the amazing Sir Roger Hunt!
Shanks gave our Doddy, a rather unusual role.
To distract the goalie, whenever close to goal.

To do this, Doddy would tell him a joke or two.
And make him laugh, like only Doddy can do!
The keeper would soon lose all sense of control.
Leaving Sir Roger to score many an easy goal!

And so Shankly's plan worked, game after game.
And in the record books, Sir Roger got his name!
He scored one hundred goals on one hundred pitches.
As the poor goalkeepers rolled around in stitches!

Heavenly Applause!

I hear loud rumbling noises in the sky.
Is a storm brewing the reason why?
Or are infant angels playing with toys?
Could that be the reason for the noise?

Are 97 red angels celebrating goals?
Or is Santa travelling between the poles?
Or maybe the answer that I'm looking for.
Doddy's arrived at Heaven's stage door!

The noise I think is heavenly applause.
In Heaven, Doddy is the biggest of draws!
So, I expect more noise until his encore.
Which will be in about five hours or more!

The Chuckle Muscle Knotty Ash Gym

Hello, Missus, are your chuckle muscles in trim?
If not, please enrol in my Knotty Ash gym.
And if your 'old mans' are starting to sag.
I'll tone them up in no time with many a gag!

My methods are unusual it'd be fair to say.
No Barbells in *this* Gym to lift and weigh!
I just do my long routine on the gym floor.
Then your chuckle muscles will grow for sure!

Don't let your chuckle muscles wither and die.
So come on in, Missus, give my gym a Diddy try.
And best of all, every session comes free.
That's how important your happiness is to me!

Wear this T-shirt, in Knotty Ash it's all the rage.
In comes in all styles and colours, to fit any age.
Read the slogan, Missus, you know it rings so true.
So don't let such a thing, ever happen to you!

A Naturally Funny Man!

Not just a comedian, much more than that!
He could make you laugh at the drop of a hat!
A naturally funny man, on or off the stage.
With a joke for every occasion, for every age!
Doddy made me laugh, when I was getting fuel.
Always good natured, never offensive or cruel.
Touring the country, north, east, south and west.
The King of Comedy, master of mirth and jest!
Doddy made people happy across the land.
With or without the need of script in hand.
Doddy had a natural gift, one he loved to share.
To make people happy just about everywhere!
A naturally funny man was Doddy, that's a fact.
To Doddy, being so funny wasn't simply an act!

Doddymas 2021!

Doddymas, Doddymas, Doddymas is here!
Let's celebrate the legend of Doddy this year!
Let's remember the king of stage and screen.
The funniest comic, the world has ever seen!

A brilliant singing voice, a ventriloquist too.
And the best ever guest star in Dr Who!
It's Doddymas, Doddymas, let's all celebrate.
The entertainer who always kept fans up late!

But those late-night shows were loved by all.
Except sleepy taxi drivers, waiting for a call!
This Doddymas, it will be such an awful shame.
If on the telly schedule, we don't see his name.

The nation would love to see a Doddy repeat.
'An Audience with Ken Dodd', a Christmas treat!
We have lots of Doddy on YouTube and tape.
The perfect watch to unwind, relax and escape!

But our Doddy's legacy is of such mass appeal.
He should be on primetime telly, reel on reel.
Because nobody like Doddy has that unique gift.
To bring a nation together and give them a lift.

So come on TV executives, do the right thing.
Imagine how much happiness Doddy will bring!
Doddy's humour is cherished across the land.
Our Doddy and Christmas telly go hand in hand!

The Famous Knotty Ash

The welcome sign, not many a word.
Just the 24 letters and a Liver Bird.
A sign you will see, by foot or by car.
It lets you know in Knotty Ash you are.

So what to expect, now you are there?
Of the Diddymen, you must be aware!
So be on the lookout wherever you go.
You might just see Dicky Mint and co!

He is only Diddy, so keep eyes peeled.
Have a jam butty from Knotty Ash yield.
The tastiest jam butty you will ever eat.
Everything in Knotty Ash is such a treat!

Knotty Ash the home of a famous squire.
So much in lovely Knotty Ash to admire!
Why is this place famous across the land?
Visit Knotty Ash, you'll soon understand!

The Knotty Ash Cinema

The Knotty Ash Cinema is one of a kind.
But as huge Doddy fans, we don't mind!
A lovely old building, off Dicky Mint Lane.
Posters of Doddy, fill every windowpane!

Outside in big letters, blue, red and white.
It says, 'A Doddy show on here tonight'.
'What's unique about that?' I hear you say.
Well, they show that same sign every day!

You see, this is a cinema in honour of Ken.
It screens Doddy footage every day till ten.
Classic TV shows, that will never grow old.
On a big silver screen... Doddy comedy gold!

Fans can choose their favourite shows too!
Double or triple bills, shown just for you!
Take the old man, Missus, give him a treat.
Pretend its 1920 and sit in the back seat!

Jam butties and repaired biccies are free.
Bring your own flask, Missus, fill it with tea!
Extra sound-proofed walls, you know why!
Too much loud laughter, decibels too high!

Such laughter could be heard in Old Swan.
And typically, most shows went on and on!
I love this cinema, it's the best in the land.
I'm off there now, with a Diddy ticket in hand.

An Empty Stage

On an empty stage, lies the Knotty Ash drum.
Another Happiness Show over of non-stop fun.
Red and blue and tickling sticks, I see a pair.
They have been waved all night, in the air.
But, those ticking sticks will be waved no more.
Doddy has left the stage that he was born for.
Those stage props famous throughout the land.
Ticking sticks once waved by the jester's hand.
The Great Drum pounded for the very last time.
The stage lights dimmed, no longer to shine.
A microphone stands alone, a sad image complete.
No more Happiness Show laughs, from every seat.

All Part of the Show!

Just seen Doddy and Dicky Mint on TV.
The very best 'Vent' act you will ever see!
They made you laugh; they made you cry.
Such a unique pair was the reason why!
Certain words, Dicky struggled to say.
And the alphabet backwards, haha, no way!
Some song lyrics, he had trouble with too!
And we know Dicky Mint couldn't say 'glue'
Tricky replies, Dicky would cleverly avoid.
At times both of them would get annoyed!
All part of the act, they loved each other so.
Winding each other up, all part of the show!
We'll never see such an act again for sure.
If only we could all see them live once more.

A Head Start!

His funny faces gave Doddy a head start!
Doddy was certainly born to play the part.
The part of jester, of top comic and fool.
To play such parts he possessed every tool.

Let's not forget Doddy, the ventriloquist too!
Dicky Mint and our Doddy, a magical brew.
But even more strings Doddy had to his bow.
A beautiful singing voice, a part of his show.

A fantastic all-rounder, so rarely seen today.
Doddy even excelled in a Shakespeare play!
So many happy memories I have to recall.
Our beloved Doddy was a cut above them all!

Diddy Parade Avenue, Liverpool 14

New houses built on Diddy Parade.
From Diddy bricks, each house is made.
The roof is Diddy and the garden too.
Of Knotty Ash, it's a got a lovely view!

It's got a Diddy gate and a Diddy wall.
One person is building it, yes, that's all!
It won't take him long, just an hour or so.
Because everything in this house is low!

He started work at 9... be finished by 10.
This is a house built for the Diddymen!
It has their names next to the Diddy bell.
A house built close to the treacle well!

The house only needs Diddy door frames.
And of course, just Diddy windowpanes!
Big street signs on Diddy Parade, it has got.
Because on Google Maps, it's hard to spot!

City of Liverpool
DIDDY PARADE
AVENUE
L14

Where's Doddy Off To?

On Lime Street Station, off to commute.
Immaculately turned out, in tie and suit.
In his travelling bag packed for the day.
I see little Dicky Mint pointing the way!
Also peeping out the bag is a jester's hat.
Where is our Doddy travelling with that?
Tickling stick too, that goes without saying!
So, where tonight is our Doddy playing?
I think he must be appearing on a TV show.
If it was a concert date, that much I'd know!
Some lucky audience awaits, that's for sure.
Just like his every audience on every tour.
Wherever he is off, whatever city or town.
Doddy as ever, will bring that house down.

Pictures

I met Doddy a few times, in the shopping aisle.
He kindly took the time to talk to me for a while.
This was in Knotty Ash, where I lived at the time.
Just by Ken's house, his home was close to mine.

He was charming as expected, forever the gent.
He treated fans the same, wherever Doddy went.
'A man of the people', Doddy could rightly claim.
He remained the same old Doddy, despite his fame.

Fame never got to Ken, he never 'acted' the star.
One occasion I got lucky, while fuelling my car.
I bumped into Doddy and he was full of fun.
He even found time to take a call from my mum!

That really made my day, and my mum's as well.
Ken was polite and respectful, and had jokes to tell!
I had no camera with me, so no pictures to display.
But I have pictures in my mind, every single day.

The Squire Bar & Grill

The best place ever for food and drink for me.
With its rooftop view of Knotty Ash to see.
And its lovely beer garden, in shade or sun.
The best bar and grill award it's just won!

Trip Adviser give it the maximum stars too.
Great reviews from customers old and new!
I am here right now, sat in my usual seat.
I've studied the menu... now it's time to eat!

A Knotty Ash Brunch I'm served on Table 9.
Washed down with the finest L14 wine!
I am with my granddaughter Alba today.
After her Diddy meal, in the garden we'll play.

On the rooftop, the grownups relax and chill.
With its splendid view from the bar and grill.
Named after Doddy... the Knotty Ash Squire.
Yet another place in Knotty Ash we all admire!

That Happy Sound!

They celebrate New Year in Heaven too.
Up there tonight there's an orderly queue.
Angels await patiently with ticket in hand.
To see the funniest man ever in the land.
Doddy is the entertainer they wait to see.
A late night for the audience it's sure to be!
And if we all listen carefully on Earth below.
We might hear the laughter from his show!
Because laughter follows Ken Dodd around.
He was gifted to spread that happy sound!

My Boyhood Hero

Doddy made you feel like he was your mate.
I felt that way as we talked at his garden gate!
Doddy was a 'people's man', nobody to shun.
He respected his fans, the all-time master of fun!

Hit records too, The Beatles he once outsold!
Ken earned discs of platinum, silver and gold.
Doddy had audiences in the palm of his hand.
Every joke Ken fired; on target it would land!

As a boy he was my hero, I loved him on TV.
To see Doddy on stage meant so much to me!
To meet him in person was even a bigger thrill.
Sir Ken Dodd, my boyhood hero, is my hero still!

Knotty Ash TV Studio

Knotty Ash TV studio, I can see its mast.
They show Doddy shows from the past.
In Knotty Ash, this is prime time TV.
The funniest shows that you'll ever see!
Vintage TV shows in old black and white.
Knotty Ash TV show them day and night.
And they also screen all his latter stuff.
I'm glued to the telly; I can't get enough!
Doddy with his very own television station.
Broadcast from L14, beamed to the nation.
And just for Pamela they cater for the USA!
And its free, Missus, so put your pension away!
Knotty Ash TV, the very best station for sure.
It's what our chuckle muscles are made for!

Happy!

It's hard to predict, will it be sunshine or rain?
Is a storm brewing that they've given a name?
Some things in life are so difficult to forecast.
We see the bright sky, but how long will it last?
But on certain things we can most surely rely!
No need to guess the outcome, not worth a try!
As that outcome is inevitable, not worth a bet.
It's unquestionable, no worries, no need to fret!
One thing in my life, which I'd bank on for sure.
Seeing Doddy, I was happy for four hours or more!

Five Great Scousers!

Five great scousers having a laugh and a joke.
John Lennon, of course had fun to poke!
The master of comedy and the kings of pop.
Five great scousers who made it to the top!
Five scousers with funny quips and gags to trade.
Such quick-witted humour, sharp as a blade!
There must be something in the Liverpool air.
That famous scouse wit, I hear it everywhere!
I see a laughing Doddy held aloft by the Fab Four.
Five great scousers, huge legends for evermore!

A Happy Dental Experience!

If you need a Knotty Ash dentist... visit me.
I'm located on Dicky Mint Lane... number 3.
Doddy is a patient of mine, don't you know!
He sometimes pops in before a stage show.

Doddy's teeth are part of his comic routine.
All part of those funny faces, we've all seen!
My surgery wall is full of funny Doddy pics.
Handsome pics too, waving two tickling sticks!

Once told 'fix your teeth' or you won't go far.
But Doddy went on to become a massive star!
Doddy would prove all the 'experts' wrong.
To enjoy an unrivalled career, decades long!

A dentist with a difference, I can claim to be.
I provide a happy experience, totally pain free!
You won't need anybody to hold your hand.
Because my surgery is set in Knotty Ash land!

The Queue!

Interval time, so I join the queue.
No not for the bar, but for the loo!
Same every time at a Doddy show.
Legs all crossed, can't wait to go!
Aching chuckle muscles of mine.
As I dash to find the 'Gents' sign!
Of trousers, I have got a spare pair.
And a portable dryer, not for my hair!
The risk comes when ticket bought.
A chance I might 'get caught short'!
But that's a risk I'm willing to take.
As I rush from my seat at every break!

One More Show

Just seen a variety show poster, Doddy top of the bill!
I must get myself a ticket, I hope they have some still.
Because wherever Doddy plays, it's a sell-out for sure.
Even though you might not get home until 3 or even 4!

In the audience Doddy will see many a familiar face.
Loyal and dedicated fans who follow him place to place.
To some a joke or two may be familiar, that's true!
But they never get tired of Doddy or of Dicky Mint too!

Every show remains special; the excitement never wanes.
Every show just like the first, in your memory it remains.
The first thing in the morning, make sure a ticket is mine.
I just hope they have some left, as yet no 'Sold Out' sign

But I wake up this morning, it was all *just* a Doddy dream.
I *really* did see the Doddy poster, on my internet screen.
It was a poster from a Blackpool show, many years ago.
I saw it just before bedtime, then dreamt of one more show.

Our Knotty Ash Currency

Knotty Ash has its own currency you know.
And our income tax rate is kept very low!
In fact, we can claim it's the best rate around.
By Jove, Missus, it's just a penny in the pound!

Our coins are diddy, but they're made of gold.
Gold from a Knotty Ash mine, so we are told.
Alas finally one day, long ago the gold ran out.
Then 'we've discovered jam' went up the shout.

Doddy appears on our currency, coin or note.
On paper money, wearing a red moggy skin coat!
On the coins, Doddy and Dicky both have a side.
Put a coin in the Diddy Train, and go for a ride!

So if you're a visitor to this neck of the woods.
And want to buy souvenirs or Knotty Ash goods.
In the Bank of Knotty Ash, do a currency swap.
And then visit Dicky Mint's diddy souvenir shop!

The Knotty Ash Treacle Tart

Ever tried a Knotty Ash Treacle Tart?
No, Missus, well it's time to start!
So, listen up all you Knotty Ash folks.
We're cracking eggs today, *not* jokes!

Be prepared for a plumptious taste.
First, tie a Doddy apron to your waist!
Then beat the eggs, until they are done.
Just like beating the Knotty Ash Drum!

Get rid of all those little diddy shells.
Then add some treacle from the wells.
Add some butter, flour and lemon zest.
Mix and bake, around an hour is best.

Turn your oven up to maximum heat.
Call Dicky Mint around to share this treat.
Have a famous jam butty while you wait.
Then let cool, and serve onto your plate!

Knotty Ash New Year Celebrations (2022)

The sky lights up over Knotty Ash.
Fireworks galore, flash after flash.
Exploding fireworks met with cheer.
As in L14, we welcome the New Year.

Among the celebrations and fun.
I fondly remember our favourite son.
The much-missed Ken Dodd, I mean.
The funniest man there has ever been!

And in these parts, he's treasured so.
He put this area on the map, you know!
So, as the year 2022, we now let in.
Let's take a moment to remember him.

**Thank you so much to Margaret @Peter Kaye photography
in Liverpool for supplying these 3 lovely photos
of a very handsome and dapper Sir Ken Dodd!**

Peter Kaye Photography

Peter Kaye Photography

CHAPTER 3

The Liverpool Echo Published Poetry

The *Liverpool Echo* has been very kind to me over the years and has published dozens of my poems on its Letters Page.

Many of these poems have been about important topics close to my heart, such as the Hillsborough disaster on 15 April 1989.

The *Echo* has also published several of my poems written about Sir Ken Dodd; a few of them appeared in my *Absent Friends* compilation Doddy tribute book.

Since that publication was released, the *Echo* has kindly published five more of my Doddy tribute poems, and that is what you'll find in this chapter.

Your Poems

A Two-Way Street

NOBODY yet has stepped up to the plate.
To see a funnier comedian, still I wait.
It's now been a year since our sad news.
Is any entertainer up to filling his shoes?

Doddy was a special breed, that's a fact
Born to entertain, with a lasting impact.
A perfected show, a stunning work of art.
A dedicated pro, which stood him apart.

Ken turned comedy into a serious craft.
Young and old, for decades we laughed.
And now a year later since our sad loss.
Doddy's still king, "The guv'nor", the boss!

Off stage, too, Doddy was one of a kind.
Time for his fans he would always find
So much mutual respect a two-way street.
Nobody with Doddy could ever compete!

Mike Bartram, L25

Your Poem

A Jam Butty Memory

I had a jam butty today for my snack.
I felt nostalgic and got thinking back.
I remember in Knotty Ash, years ago.
When I was a young lad, about five or
so.

I had Ken Dodd wallpaper on my wall.
A big Diddymen fan, since I was small.
On my wallpaper was a jam butty mine.
And on such butties, I loved to dine!

I was told, jam butty mines were real.
Where they were, Mum wouldn't
reveal!
A secret that the Diddymen would
keep.
But I did find them, in my dreamy
sleep!
by Mike Bartram, L25

Your Poem

The Last Diddyman

Walking the sands for evermore.
I saw a Diddyman on the shore.
In Blackpool he walked all alone.
Liverpool lad, Knotty Ash his home.
But Knotty Ash now not the same.
I said 'hello' Dicky Mint his name.
Dicky all forlorn by the rolling sea.
He turned saying 'hello' back to me.
I saw a tear fall from his diddy eye.
Doddy I said would say 'not to cry'
On a deserted beach, lights so dim.
'It's time to go home' I said to him.
So home we went, Knotty Ash bound.
The last Diddyman I now had found.

by Mike Bartram, L25

1 1 1

Lovely artwork by Daniel Hanton

Your Poem

Maybe Because It's Christmas

MAYBE because it's Christmas, we miss our
Doddy more.
No Doddy festive shows, with late-night laughs
galore.
Maybe because it's Christmas, with snowfall in
the sky.
Is the reason people turn back clocks to days
gone by.

Maybe because it's Christmas, with frost upon
the pane.
Is why I feel so nostalgic as I stroll down Thomas
Lane.
Maybe because it's Christmas, beautiful carols to
hear.
Is why we miss absent friends more at this time
of year.

Maybe because it's Christmas, with Santa upon
his sleigh.
Is why Doddy followers today, put a quiet
moment away.
So as Christmas is upon us and "Happiness" fills
the air.
We wish a Merry Christmas to our departed
Squire and Sir.

by Michael Bartram

113

Your Poem

We All Live...

We all live near a jam butty mine.
Not far from the Knotty Ash sign.
We all live near a sticky treacle well.
Close to the sound of a factory bell.
A factory where biccies they mend.
By Brookside Avenue, off the bend.
We all live near a moggy skin ranch.
The only one, a Knotty Ash branch!
We all live near the gravy train route.
Every hour we hear its happy toot!
Those snuff quarries are in our view.
And the Happiness Train passes too!
As we all live in Knotty Ash you see!
Every day I think...how lucky are we!

**By Michael Bartram (currently preparing
a book of poetry dedicated to Doddy)**

CHAPTER 4

Acrostic Style Poetry

I love the challenge 'acrostic' style poetry presents. An acrostic poem is one in which the first letter of each line read downwards spells the poem's title. This form of writing significantly narrows down the choice of words with which to open each line, hence the challenge!

In this chapter there are 12 acrostic poems dedicated to Sir Ken Dodd.

Young Man!

Yesterday was the 'official' Doddy Day.
Once a year is not enough, I would say!
Underneath the comic, a perfect gent!
Now a heavenly greeting I've just sent!
Good day, 'young man', he'd often say.

Meeting Doddy always made my day!
And I always loved how he greeted me!
Never again such a genius we will see!

We Are Doddy Fans

We are Doddy fans, Knotty Ash I'm from!
Even as a little boy, he was my number one.

All around the world, so many fans like me.
Raised on Doddy, across every land and sea.
Every Ken Dodd fan will proudly tell you so.

Doddy was the master of stage or TV show.
Off stage, Doddy was the very best too.
Discovered that myself, in a shopping queue!
Doddy was a great guy, humble and polite.
Young Emma and Rachel, loved him at first sight!

Followers of Doddy, we will forever remain.
A comedy world without him is not the same!
Nobody can replace our Doddy, it's fair to say.
So, we just recall the memories every single day!

Dickie Mint

Dickie Mint here, though diddy I am.
Inside the emotions of a ten-foot man.
Cry I still do, missing our routine to do.
Knotty Ash is not the same without you.
I miss you Doddy, in Heaven can you tell?
Every day tears drip into the Treacle Well.

Miss my mate, the great laughs we had.
I'm sorry at times for being a naughty lad!
Nobody will ever top the 'Happiness Show'
Tears for you Doddy, every day still flow.

Haha... a bit of poetic licence taken here with *Dicky's* name!

Miss You Ken

Months have passed, now Autumn is here.
It would have been a great time of year.
Summer is a memory, but *no* need to frown.
Shows of Doddy happiness, now to hit town!

You knew what to expect, the perfect show.
Only Sir Ken Dodd could entertain us so!
Uproar of laughs, deep into the night heard.

Ken, we miss you, your every funny word!
Entertainers, well, most just come and go.
Not the same, without a Doddy Autumn show!

Laughter

Laughter, Doddy gave us year on year.
A sold-out show, wherever he'd appear.
Unique in my eyes, second to none.
Gave his all on stage, from minute one.
Happiness, a gift he was born to spread.
The Diddymen of Knotty Ash, Doddy led.
Entertainer extraordinaire, Squire of L14.
Ruler forever of comic stage and screen.

The Ken Doddy Bus (The Number 10)

Travel on the 'Ken Dodd' bus if you can.
Here on a visit, make it part of your plan.
Enjoy the ride, on the route number 10.

Knotty Ash awaits you with its Diddymen.
Everyone knows this part of Liverpool 14.
Not everywhere Dicky Mint might be seen!

Don't forget your camera just in case.
One of the Diddymen you suddenly face!
Don't be surprised at what you might see.
Due might be a gravy train in time for tea!
You see Knotty Ash is not a myth, it's real.

Broken biscuit factories part of its appeal.
Use your imagination while on this bus.
Seeing a jam butty mine, will be another plus!

Another little tale of the secret UFO landing in Knotty Ash!

On Thomas Lane

Other worlds... they are out there for sure.
Not long ago, Aliens knocked on our door!

Thomas Lane then became our visitor's base.
Home now to our friends from outer space!
On a secret mission, they came on a craft.
Mick the Marmaliser, saw their light shaft.
And so, the other Diddymen, he went to tell.
So it was, a UFO landed near a treacle well!

Learning to laugh, the ET's loved Mick and co.
And as nobody else saw that cosmic glow.
No human will ever discover their secret trail.
Each Diddyman promised not to share this tale!

I Draw The Line!

I love my animals... 'No doggy...no show'!

Dogs are a man's best friend you know!
Reptiles, close up, however, I'm not so sure.
A line, while I am touring, I have to draw!
Waiting for me once in Wigan, twelve foot in size!

Taking me by shock, by complete surprise!
Hoping to share my dressing room with me.
Eye to eye with a Burmese python, I came to be!

Lost for Diddy words, but I soon found a few!
I politely stated this room is not meant for two!
No offence taken by Steve and his slippery pet.
Easily the strangest support act I had ever met!

This poem is based on a true story, told to me by Steve Nasir
(the python owner!). Steve was on the same bill as Doddy and
surprised Doddy with his dressing room companion for the
show!!

Chuckle Muscles

Chuckle muscles can't be seen on X-ray or scan.
Hysterics they cause, like only such muscles can!
Use them every day, don't allow them to rest.
Check they are working, so put them to the test.
Keep watching our Doddy, it always works for me!
Laughing is contagious, and best of all it's free!
Everyone's got a chuckle muscle, Doddy told us so.

Mine goes into overdrive, if I see a Doddy show!
Unique is the chuckle muscle, different in every way.
Some deny its existence, watch some Doddy I say!
Crying you'll be with laughter, tears upon your face.
Living proof your chuckle muscle is certainly in place!
Exercise you chuckle muscle, let laughter fill the air.
Split your sides laughing, with Doddy jokes to share!

Keep Doddy In Your Heart

Ken Dodd... we miss him every day.
Easily my biggest hero, in every way!
Even had Doddy wallpaper on my wall.
Perfect all-rounder, our Doddy had it all!

Did Knotty Ash exist, I'd ask my Mum?
Of course, she replied, it's a land of fun!
Diddymen lived there, my Mum said so.
Doddy on TV, I never missed a show!
Youth came and went, teen into a man.

In my growing-up years, I was still a fan.
Nothing has changed, not to this day.

You will not find a better comic, no way!
On the stage, from the first curtain call.
Under his magic spell we sat, one and all!
Roars of laughter heard from each show.

Happiness *and* Doddy, together did go!
Ever since Sir Ken sadly passed away.
Around the world, he is missed every day.
Rest in peace, Squire, forever we'll miss you.
The King of Comedy... that will always be true!

Funny Man

Funniest man ever, he was to me.
Ultimate professional, plain to see.
No need to offend, be mean or blue.
Never off stage until about 1 or 2!
Year after year, he toured the UK.

Making us laugh in his unique way!
And now he is gone, we miss him so.
Nobody can ever better a Doddy show!

Legend!

Liverpool legends, there are quite a few!
Every walk of life, they come from too.
Great actors, writers, comics, pop stars.
Evergreen footballers, proud they are ours!
No other city can boast what we have got.
Doddy, the King of Comedy, he tops the lot!

CHAPTER 5

Poetry with Graphic Designed Artwork

In this chapter there are 8 Doddy poems that have been superbly designed for this publication. I think such terrific designs add something very special to the written word. Thank you to the very talented people behind these designs!

City of Liverpool

DODDY PARK
KNOTTY ASH

Bonfire Night In Knotty Ash

It's Bonfire Night in Knotty Ash.
Diddy bangers with Diddy flash!
Diddy sparklers, waved in the air.
Diddy Rockets, and a Diddy flare!

In Doddy Park, a Diddy bonfire.
With a Diddy tribute to The Squire.
A Diddy spin of a Catherine Wheel.
People eating their jam butty meal!

Dicky Mint tells a funny Doddy joke.
Over Knotty Ash, some Diddy smoke.
A Fountain spurts its Diddy flame.
A Bonfire party, all in Doddy's name!

129

The Knotty Ash Easter Egg Hunt

There are Easter eggs, hidden in Knotty Ash today!
So join in the hunt, get to Liverpool 14 without delay!
Come on the Happiness Train, or Doddy Bus 10B.
It's such a beautiful day for it Missus...and it's free!

Age doesn't matter, children up to Great Grand Mum.
Knotty Ash welcomes everyone for a day of Easter fun!
There are eggs hidden near my flat in Doddy Towers.
And some in Springfield Park, amongst the flowers.

Rumour has it, in Dicky Mint Lane, eggs can be found!
And Eggs by the Treacle Well, a whisper going around!
An Easter announcement from The Town Hall Mayor.
He has hinted, in the Town Hall, eggs could be there!

Dicky Mint was seen in Little Bongs; I wonder why?
Was he hiding Easter Eggs, from his Knotty Ash supply?
I can give you these clues, but Diddy clues, that's all.
Maybe you should try searching in the Happiness Hall!

On the morning Knotty Ash beach, it's all sand no tide.
Perhaps that's a good place for Easter Eggs to hide!
Is there more than just Gravy on Sunday's Gravy Train?
Has Lady Dodd hidden some eggs on Thomas Lane?

Hunting near the Moggy Ranch is worth a good bet.
And in the Jam Butty Mines, some luck you might get!
So come along to magical Knotty Ash, this Easter time.
A very Happy Easter to the lovely Doddy friends of mine!

The Jam Butty Bus Run!

We sat upstairs, on a bus seat.
Jam butties, I was given to eat.
Not any old butties, I must add.
The best butties we've ever had!
'Why was that'? you may inquire.
Well, it was all down to the Squire!
As, Ken was our host on that bus!
Of Jimmy and I, he made a fuss!
Knotty Ash butties we were fed.
So, the very best jam and bread!
And on that Knotty Ash bus run.
We had such happiness and fun!
A jam butty party, just for us 3!
It's such a lovely memory for me.

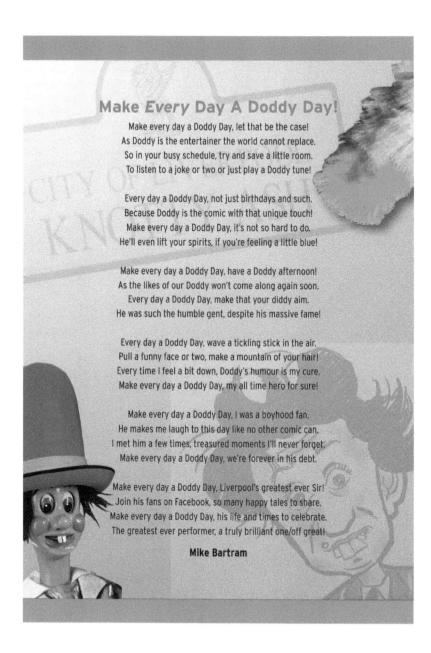

Make *Every* Day A Doddy Day!

Make every day a Doddy Day, let that be the case!
As Doddy is the entertainer the world cannot replace.
So in your busy schedule, try and save a little room.
To listen to a joke or two or just play a Doddy tune!

Every day a Doddy Day, not just birthdays and such.
Because Doddy is the comic with that unique touch!
Make every day a Doddy Day, it's not so hard to do.
He'll even lift your spirits, if you're feeling a little blue!

Make every day a Doddy Day, have a Doddy afternoon!
As the likes of our Doddy won't come along again soon.
Every day a Doddy Day, make that your diddy aim.
He was such the humble gent, despite his massive fame!

Every day a Doddy Day, wave a tickling stick in the air.
Pull a funny face or two, make a mountain of your hair!
Every time I feel a bit down, Doddy's humour is my cure.
Make every day a Doddy Day, my all time hero for sure!

Make every day a Doddy Day, I was a boyhood fan.
He makes me laugh to this day like no other comic can.
I met him a few times, treasured moments I'll never forget.
Make every day a Doddy Day, we're forever in his debt.

Make every day a Doddy Day, Liverpool's greatest ever Sir!
Join his fans on Facebook, so many happy tales to share.
Make every day a Doddy Day, his life and times to celebrate.
The greatest ever performer, a truly brilliant one/off great!

Mike Bartram

Dr 'Doddy' Who

I always thought Doddy would make a great Dr Who.
Intellectual, a bit scatty and a sense of humour too!
Dicky Mint, the perfect assistant by Doddy's side.
Through the Universe, together in the Tardis to ride!

From all the perils and dangers they would face,
They would come away laughing from outer space!
Those dreaded Daleks, our Doddy could easily tame.
Their deadly extermination powers would be in vain!

Doddy would soon have his enemies under his thumb.
Not even a Dalek could resist Doddy's sense of fun!
The Yeti and the Cyberman, would be a threat no more.
As they would be under Doddy's magical spell for sure!

The Teeth!

Doddy stands on the Blackpool sand.
A huge bar of Blackpool Rock in hand!
But don't take a bite Doddy, only a lick!
Don't be tempted to munch that stick!

Those teeth are precious, that's a fact.
A very funny, important part of the act!
In your insurance policy, paragraph 2.
It states 'Blackpool Rock, do not chew'

As your teeth might chip, with just 1 bite!
So any temptation to nibble, please fight!
Pose with the Rock, a great publicity shot.
But to sneak a Diddy bite...definitely not!

'Mr Liverpool'

'Mr Liverpool'...what a proud title to own!
To be so loved in your City, your home.
Who deserves such an honour to receive?
Only one man it could be, I truly believe!

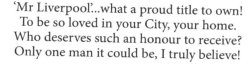

Could it be 'Macca' cos I love Beatle Paul?
Or a local footy icon, with a big medal haul?
Of possibilies, I've got quite a long list!
But that special ingredient in most is missed.

A person to his roots who stayed so true.
A humble scouser, even when fame grew.
A dignified gentleman, it would help to be.
And the greatest entertainer, we'll ever see!

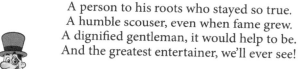

For 'Mr Liverpool' only one man fits that bill.
My hero as a young child and my hero still.
A person so respected within our City walls.
On Sir Ken Dodd, this prestigious tile falls!

But what about Dicky Mint, I hear you ask?
He was Doddy's bezzie, and up to every task.
And I agree, he deserves his own title too.
So why not share it...that's what best mates do!

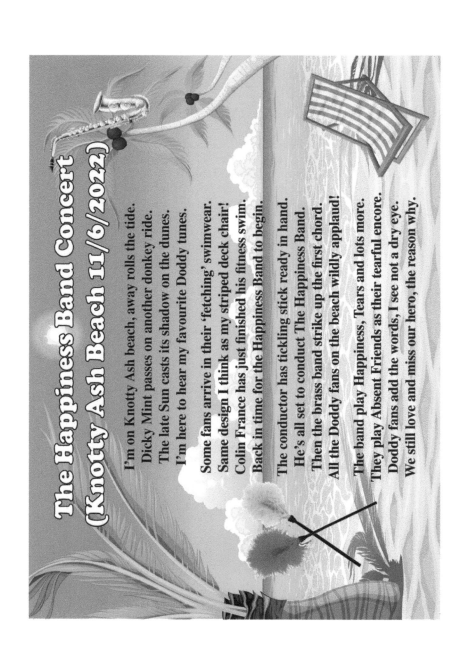

The Happiness Band Concert
(Knotty Ash Beach 11/6/2022)

I'm on Knotty Ash beach, away rolls the tide.
Dicky Mint passes on another donkey ride.
The late Sun casts its shadow on the dunes.
I'm here to hear my favourite Doddy tunes.

Some fans arrive in their 'fetching' swimwear.
Same design I think as my striped deck chair!
Colin France has just finished his fitness swim.
Back in time for the Happiness Band to begin.

The conductor has tickling stick ready in hand.
He's all set to conduct The Happiness Band.
Then the brass band strike up the first chord.
All the Doddy fans on the beach wildly applaud!

The band play Happiness, Tears and lots more.
They play Absent Friends as their tearful encore.
Doddy fans add the words, I see not a dry eye.
We still love and miss our hero, the reason why.

CHAPTER 6

Poetry (Including Fans' Artwork)

'International Happiness Day'!
(20 March 2022)

It's 'Happiness Day' so lots of laughs to raise!
Unless sadly, you are having 'one of those days'!
But if you are and you've nothing else planned.
Then all is not lost… there is some help at hand!
Listen to our Doddy, dig out an old DVD or tape.
For those such days it will be the perfect escape!
'An Audience with Ken Dodd' that is a great start.
Follow that show up with the funny second part!
Or just log on to YouTube, it's full of Doddy fun.
You're sure to feel happy when your day is done!
Then you'll feel a part of this special happy day.
As Doddy has that gift to wipe the blues away!
On this international celebration, an idea from me!
Doddy for its figurehead, how fitting that would be!

'Broke The Mould'

If you were to ask me, and the truth be told.
I'd say in making Doddy they 'broke the mould'.
Because only one Doddy there could ever be.
The original and best for the world to see!
A one-city man, who stuck close to his roots.
Ambitious and successful in his many pursuits.
A gentleman scholar, from almost bygone days.
Never afraid to be different in so many ways.
With his loyal fans, he created a special bond.
Took entertainment to a new level, and beyond.
Could you ever imagine another Doddy type act?
I don't think that's possible and that's a fact!
Such an impossible act to follow, it seems unfair.
Yes, they 'broke that mould', no argument there!

Liverpool's 'Finest' Goalkeeper!

About to play football in his red-and-white attire.
Emerging from the tunnel, the Knotty Ash Squire!
Onto the pitch runs the funniest man in the land!
He heads towards the Kop goal with ball in hand.
Doddy was sporting his famous mop of mad hair.
He made himself look daft, but Doddy didn't care!
As to spread 'happiness' was his ultimate aim.
To put some sunshine in our day to replace the rain.
So in the Spion Kop goal, Doddy has shots to face.
Doddy dived everywhere... except the right place!
Some of Shankly's boys can be seen laughing away.
They are watching the funniest ever keeper display!
Isn't that just Doddy all over, a laugh a minute treat!
Even on a football pitch, his antics impossible to beat!

A Chuckle Muscle Problem!

I went to the doctors today in Thomas Lane.
Although I wasn't hurting and I wasn't in pain.
But my chuckles muscles worked no more.
So I went to my doctors, looking for the cure.

'Sit down,' the doctor said, 'and take a seat.'
But first the doctor gave me a jam butty to eat.
Then I sat myself down in the patient's chair.
And told the doctor my problem and my despair.

'Don't worry, young man,' he said, 'help is at hand.'
Though this is a rare problem in Knotty Ash land!
He said 'Go down to the DVD shop straight away.
'And hand over this prescription without delay.'

On my doctor's prescription, this is what it said.
'Watch twice a day, morning and again before bed.'
So, I did exactly what my doctor told me to do.
I watched 'An Audience With Doddy', parts 1 and 2.

Today is a new day, the morning sunny and bright.
My doctor's advice was perfect, he got it so right!
As I head to work in the famous jam butty mine.
My chuckle muscles cured, now working overtime!

The 3 Princesses of Knotty Ash

The Princesses of Knotty Ash, there are 3!
As our Doddy 'knighted' them on bended knee.
Tickling stick tapped on shoulders, left and right.
A special memory to forever cherish and delight.
The 3 Princesses of Knotty Ash they became.
One moment with Doddy… one lifetime of fame!
Now wherever the girls go, they will forever be.
A Princess of Knotty Ash for the world to see.
That is an honour no amount of money can buy.
And all because of Sir Ken Dodd, the reason why!

A true story folks!

**A beautiful picture… Amie, Emma and Lucy Potter,
the 3 Princesses of Knotty Ash**

Doddy's Style

A British sense of humour, at its very best.
Ken was the master, a cut above the rest.
Cheeky seaside postcards, brought to life.
Jokes about blondes, in-laws and the wife!

All harmless fun, a 'play on words' or two.
No vulgarity and nothing remotely blue.
Nobody to embarrass, insult or to offend.
That was Doddy's style, right until the end.

Doddy had crafted the perfect stage show.
An audience in his palm, and not letting go!
Into the early hours, on would go the fun.
That's why a nation's heart Doddy had won!

Worth Every Trip!

Big Doddy fan, Pamela from the USA.
Has travelled this week to the UK.
She travelled on a Doddy Airline plane.
Then she caught the Happiness Train.

So, is she jet lagged, I don't think so?
As she's already off to a Doddy show!
She's made this trip many times before.
And every time, well worth it for sure!

Whether by air, or across the sea on ship.
To see and meet Doddy, worth every trip!
Doddy of course, made the perfect host.
That is why, we respect Doddy the most!

The Clock and Doddy

Just seen a picture of Doddy after his show.
One big happy audience, all off home to go.
But the last bus home, will no longer be there!
As the echoes of laughter still ring in the air.
The clock in the background caught my eye!
The time it was displaying, the reason why.
Almost 2.30 in the morning, that was the time.
And that's the reason Doddy's a hero of mine.
Still greeting his fans, though the hour was late.
This was our Doddy all over, such a lovely trait.
Doddy loved his audience, uniquely so, I'd say.
We loved him back, and still do, to this very day!

Myth or Reality?

As you leave the busy area of Old Swan.
You enter a land where Diddymen are from.
You'll be in Knotty Ash, worldwide known.
The finest place ever, to call your home.

The place to let your imagination run wild.
The place I loved when I was a young child.
The place I watched my young children grow.
So many memories, and I love them all so!

In The Greyhound I celebrated our Cup win!
In Springfield Park, I played with puppy Kim.
In Sainsbury's, I met Doddy, I won't forget that.
He looked all dapper in his long coat and hat!

The home of a drum that doesn't need a band.
The most famous big drum across the land!
The magic of Knotty Ash, you can almost feel.
Be myth or reality, *you* can choose what's real!

My Diddy Knotty Ash Dream

Last night I enjoyed a Knotty Ash dream.
I sailed a Diddy boat down a Diddy stream.
I climbed Diddy trees in Springfield Park.
In beautiful Little Bongs, it never got dark.

In Knotty Ash Airport, landed a Diddy plane.
I saw Dickie Mint walk down Thomas Lane.
And in Alder Hey all the children were well.
On Knotty Ash TV, Doddy had jokes to tell.

On Brookside Avenue, I saw my old home.
No people in my dream were fully grown!
At Knotty Ash Diddy Station, platform 5.
I saw a packed Happiness Train slowly arrive.

In Knotty Ash harbour, full of Diddy boats.
I noticed everybody wore moggy skin coats!
And in this blissful, dreamy Knotty Ash land.
Everyone I saw, had jam butties in their hand!

Continuing from the 'UFO Over Knotty Ash' poems earlier in the book, please find here the third and final part of this Diddy series of poems. The first poem is written in a style that I have never tried before (AAAA), in which all four lines of each verse share the same rhyme.

I love the subject of this sci-fi poem, but can't bring myself to like this format too much, so I consider this poem a one-off attempt at writing in such a way!

My Cuppa With An Alien!

I took an Alien home with me for tea.
Looking just like anyone else you'll see!
His secret will always be safe with me.
In Knotty Ash, Aliens there'll always be!

Because they came here late last May.
And loved it so much, decided to stay.
From outer space they made their way.
And set their sights on Knotty Ash Bay.

The Aliens had seen new worlds unfold.
Seen the death of planets put on hold.
But now they were getting weary and old.
Suffered too many winters, long and cold.

They had never heard laughter before.
It didn't exist in their own world for sure!
They'd seen everything to see and more.
Seen worlds at peace and worlds at war.

Cont.

149

And so to planet Earth they chose to fly.
Just another world they were passing by.
They landed in Knotty Ash from up high.
To see how we lived, was their reason why.

The Aliens will be forever in Doddy's debt.
He had them laughing as soon as they met!
Then they made a decision, never to regret.
To stay in Knotty Ash, their heart was set!.

After watching the Doddy Happiness Show.
They discovered laughter, all its joy and glow.
When time to go home, they chose not to go.
In Knotty Ash, their chuckle muscles did grow!

Now with my Alien friend, a cuppa we share.
With broken biscuits that were beyond repair.
I share Knotty Ash tales about its famous Sir.
My friend's giggles and laughter filled the air!

No Chance Meeting

I took a stroll around Knotty Ash today.
I was slightly emotional; I have to say.
From Doddy's home, I was merely yards.
Alas, no chance meeting was on the cards.

I saw the church where Doddy would pray.
Just a minute's walk from the new Alder Hey.
I went to Sainsbury's, some shopping to do.
Sadly, I won't see our Doddy in the queue.

Reflecting, I walked up and down each aisle.
I thought of The Squire, it made me smile.
I bumped into Doddy here a few years ago.
Did he make me laugh, that answer you know!

I then got the bus home, I jumped the 10B.
Not the Arriva 'Doddy Bus' I was hoping to see!
Some fantastic memories, I have for sure.
A shame I don't live in Knotty Ash anymore.

The Gravy Train To Ainsdale Mission!

In Ainsdale, close to the Southport resort.
Of gravy, we hear they are running short.
It's Sunday, and many lunches to prepare.
Lunch plates without gravy… far too bare!

This was a crisis, so without further delay.
Help is called for, and it's soon on the way!
A Diddy call to Knotty Ash is made quick.
'Have you any gravy to spare, thin or thick?'

'The gravy trains have nearly a full supply.'
Came the Knotty Ash Gravy Train reply.
So eager to help, and without further ado.
The Gravy Train quickly left from platform 2.

With lots of lovely Knotty Ash gravy onboard.
The Gravy Train to Ainsdale quickly roared!
The grateful Ainsdale folk hadn't long to wait
Before that gravy soon arrived on their plate!

KEN DODD'S
DIDDYMEN
THE GRAVY TRAIN

A BIG TELEVISION BOOK

Rainbow

I'm sitting here this Sunday at a loose end.
So, I likened a Rainbow to our absent friend.
Rainbows are colourful, that wonderful arc.
Once in the sky, they always leave their mark.
When a storm moves on, they lift the gloom.
Just like a flower in the sky in summer bloom.
That's just like our Doddy, you have to say.
He had the gift to brighten up our every day!
Rainbows are magical, a bit hard to explain.
A one-off phenomenon, our Doddy's the same!
So next time I see a rainbow, each colour, all seven.
I'll dedicate it to our absent friend in Heaven.

My House-warming Party!

There's a party in my flat in a few hours.
A house-warming party in Doddy Towers.
It's an open invitation… I invite you all.
But if you're coming, please give me a call.

Just so I know that I have enough bread.
And enough jam from the mines to spread!
Come to Knotty Ash, by air, road or boat.
The Happiness Train is full, please take note!

Fully booked, Missus, has been for a while.
It's the best way to travel, to arrive in style!
If you are local, catch the Doddy Bus 10B.
That bus stops just a Diddy walk from me.

Dicky Mint is coming; he's informed me so.
And on my big telly, lots of Doddy to show!
So please come along, there's no dress code.
I want to see happy faces, by the truck load!

A Man of Many Parts

Doddy read out, 'She's 111, I mean she's ill!'
Now sadly left us, but the funniest man still.
Jokes fired at an audience at a torpedo rate.
Getting home from his shows, ever so late!

No need to shock, embarrass or to outrage.
Just the best act ever to adorn the stage!
The Knotty Ash Guvnor, legend and Squire.
Up and coming comics he will always inspire.

From Doddy, young comics will forever learn.
But our audience is over, now it's God's turn.
We miss you Doddy, with all of our hearts.
The ultimate entertainer, a man of many parts!

The 'Sailing Ship Doddy'

In Knotty Ash harbour, boats sail or rest.
Just like the airport, it's the nation's best!
Boats head for the Mersey or the Irish Sea.
Like all in this wonderful land, travel is free!
The Diddymen of course, make up the crew.
Dicky Mint is in charge, that's nothing new!
He's the captain of SS *Doddy*, what a boat.
As I watch her into the harbour, quietly float.
There are images of Doddy on stern and bow.
And only happy passengers, such boats allow!
For a happy day out, from Knotty Ash they sail.
And onboard, Doddy fans share many a tale!
Sailing in calm waters or riding a Diddy wave.
Doddy fans recall all the great times he gave!

Always Room

No sooner has the ink on my pen run dry.
And another Doddy poem comes quickly by!
It's not possible to run out of things to say.
Especially when I'm down Knotty Ash way!
I could write about his humour or his voice.
Or about his ventriloquist act, what a choice!
And Doddy the intellect deserves a few lines.
Or about when I met him, my favourite times!
One man, many topics, and so much range.
Instantly his act, my mood he could change!
Not many people, if any at all, spring to mind.
Have inspired me so much with words to find.
And hopefully that won't end anytime soon.
And for one more poem, there is *always* room.

The Busy Diddymen

I passed by Doddy's home, no Diddymen in view.
They must be all at work, they all have jobs to do!
To the famous Jam Butty Mines they have to tend.
Down the snuff quarries, so much time to spend.

Those gravy trains have to keep running on time.
Broken biscuits to be fixed on the production line.
Don't forget the Moggy Ranch, very busy in there.
Only place to purchase a moggy skin coat to wear!

But the Diddymen love to be busy, they told me so!
Be in the Knotty Ash sunshine, the rain or snow.
Busy on Black Pudding Plantation, they'd rather be.
As it helps with the pain of missing Doddy, you see.

Postcard to Heaven

A postcard from our Doddy was dispatched.
It came today with a heavenly stamp attached.
So, I thought we'd send Doddy a little reply.
Just about life in general as these days go by.
Well, the Blackpool Sea and the sands still meet.
At Anfield, Liverpool FC are still hard to beat!
There are Christmas movies already on the TV.
Despite the Halloween parties are still yet to be!
Our new tribute book for you, that's nearly done.
And every day in Knotty Ash still rises the sun.
Trees in the autumn winds still sway and bend.
And every day we still miss our absent friend.
So, all in all, Doddy, life is pretty much the same.
Except of course, that is life on Thomas Lane.
I still pass by your house almost every day.
A certain magic is missing around Knotty Ash way.
This postcard in return, we send to Heaven above.
From your fans and Diddymen, with all our love.

Mr Universe Contest 1973

Will you come back in time with me?
To the Mr Universe Contest of 1973.
Lots of muscular type poses to make.
The World Championship Cup is at stake!

But *what's this*, a late entry, number14.
With the *biggest* muscles ever seen!
Enter the Squire, Ken Dodd into the fray.
With the stand out muscles of the day!

Bulging muscles, Missus, front and back.
With an impressive Chuckle Muscle 6 pack!
Muscles developed over a brilliant career.
Laughing his head off, each day of the year!

But Doddy's Chuckle Muscles are not unique.
Use *yours* daily to get the same physique!
Doddy easily won the contest, hands down.
For the King of Comedy, yet *another* Crown!

(**Well done Doddy, a deserved winner, I *did* come a distant
second though!**)

Happy and Carefree

If you're ever up Knotty Ash way.
Be sure to stop... 'Hello' to say.
Folk will greet you, with tip of hat.
Yes, Knotty Ash is just like that!
And if you want, I will be your guide.
Take you on a Happiness Train ride!
Show you around our famous land.
Today, if you have nothing planned!
To the Jam Butty Mines we will go.
And so much more for you to show.
Everyone here is happy and carefree.
And Dicky Mint you're bound to see!
Take home happy snaps of your tour.
A place like you've never seen before!

Springfield Park Garden Fete

Today is the Knotty Ash Garden Fete.
It's going to be busy, so don't be late!
So, to Springfield Park, I make my way.
In Knotty Ash, yet another special day!

Opening the fete, a very special host.
The pride of Knotty Ash, it can boast!
The one and only Ken Dodd of course.
When it comes to comedy, what a force!

And Dicky Mint will be attending as well.
I'm so happy and excited, can't you tell!
The advertising posters, promise much.
Jam butty stalls, Diddy rides and such!

Take a penalty against Doddy in goal.
Diddy golf course, haha, only one hole!
Fresh Treacle Well products for us to buy.
Fixed biscuits sale next to a coconut shy!

Buy some raffle tickets, be in the draw.
Today L14 is the best place to be for sure!
The main appeal, a Doddy 'Meet and Greet'
So, meet Sir Ken, make your day complete!

Love Him Still

Hey Doddy, a message from us fans to you!
We're writing a new book, book number two.
As so many more tributes have been made.
So many more compliments have been paid!
Stories, poetry, with lots of artwork sublime.
We still remember our Doddy all of the time!
The world of entertainment is not the same.
No new tour posters, which show your name.
We miss getting home from your show so late.
We miss your double act with your best mate!
We miss you on stage, the radio and on TV.
As nobody can replace you, that is plain to see!
Another tribute book for Doddy is easy to fill
As colleagues, fans and media, love him still!

Same Time Tomorrow?

To a Jam Butty Mine he was making his way.
'Hello, Dicky,' I said, 'how are you today?'
'Can I come along too and share the walk?'
'Of course,' said Dicky, 'I could do with a talk.'

Along the Knotty Ash roads, we made stride.
Doddy's best mate, Dicky Mint, by my side.
I saw a factory with broken biscuits to repair.
In snuff quarries, I saw other Diddymen there.

Dicky spoke to me on the way to the mine.
He sadly asked me, 'Why was it Doddy's time?
'I miss him so much, our happy, funny routine.'
I said, 'Sometimes, Dicky, God has to intervene.'

Dicky Mint agreed, he knew that was the case.
And I saw a tear trickle down his Diddy face.
At the Jam Butty Mine, Dicky said his goodbye.
'Same time tomorrow,' I said. 'Yes please,' his reply.

"When you said The Show finished at 20-45, I didn't
know you meant *the Year*"!!
Haha...Ring a bell anyone? Love this brilliant
artwork by Gladys Chucklebutty

The Knotty Ash Gravy Train

From the Gravy Train to your plate.
Hardly any time, you'll have to wait.
The best gravy ever we can boast.
For all your meals and Sunday roast!

The Gravy Train runs from Knotty Ash.
With your gravy needs on your mash.
The Gravy Train stops at Broadgreen.
Close to my Rachel's house, in L14.

A lovely Diddy area, the best around.
Where Doddy's house can be found.
We deliver it hot, right to your home.
So don't buy Bisto or Tesco's own!

On your chips, Missus, give it a try.
It's from Knotty Ash, the reason why!
An area full of magic, fun and mystique.
A happy land, every day of the week!

The Woolton Cinema Doddy Event!
(18 November 2018)

To Woolton Liverpool, Doddy fans descend.
The city of our much-missed absent friend.
A cinema event to screen his hilarious show.
Ken may even be watching, you never know!

Don't throw your cinema ticket into the bin.
It's also a free raffle ticket, great prizes to win!
Keyrings, plaques and a retro shopping bag.
And a star prize, an autographed Doddy mag!

I only wish The Squire could be with us today.
Making us all laugh in his special, unique way!
This event we hold, a tribute to the great man.
If you've a spare minute, Ken, join us if you can!

171

Happy Birthday Squire

Happy Birthday Doddy... life's not quite the same.
We need a laugh right now, during this Covid pain.
Who better to raise our spirits in this current clime?
Than the funniest man I've known in my lifetime.
But I guess with hilarious memories I'll have to do.
Because nobody could ever take the place of you!
But if only you were here to help lift the gloom.
And lighten these times with a Doddy joke or tune!
'Doddy Day' was yesterday, but so is today for me!
'Happy Birthday Squire'... my hero you'll always be.

The 'Cafe Doddy'

If you want to treat yourself and eat out.
Try the cafe Doddy' by the roundabout.
Opening hours every day, from 8 till 3.
Biscuits have been fixed to dip in your tea!
For the main course try bangers and mash.
The very best sausage, Missus, in Knotty Ash!
Or if your boss is treating you on your break.
Then you must try our scrumptious steak!
If lunch is on you, buy a butty, egg or ham.
All the produce is local, the gravy and jam!
The black pudding is fresh; the treacle is too.
To all our lovely tourists, try our scouse stew.
It's the very best cafe in Liverpool 14.
So, visit 'Cafe Doddy' to see what I mean!

Doddy Plays Doddy at
The Knotty Ash Grand!

Closed, are all the local factory floors.
Not revolving are the L14 shop doors!
Everyone has gone to the theatre today.
To see the opening of a new Doddy play.

A play in which Doddy plays himself.
Tickets, like hot cakes, flew of the shelf!
It's not on Broadway or the West End.
As this play is special, it bucks the trend!

This show opens at The Knotty Ash Grand.
All Knotty Ash folk, have tickets in hand!
I take my seat, in middle row of the stalls.
The band play Happiness, the curtain falls.

Cue rapturous applause, I rise to my feet.
And everyone else has risen from their seat!
The Knotty Ash roads are empty, bar none.
As we are all in this theatre, awaiting Act 1!

A Heavenly Place

One year ago, our final respects to pay.
People of all ages gathered that day.
I saw grown men there not afraid to cry.
To a Liverpool legend we said 'Goodbye.'

It was a bitter day with the threat of rain.
Laughter was mixed with sorrow and pain.
The service on big screens was relayed.
As moving tributes were lovingly made.

In the cathedral's shadow that afternoon.
A tear was followed by another one soon.
To a heavenly place our Doddy had gone.
As the service closed the sun now shone.

Ola Ness conducted the concert band.
Not with baton, but tickling stick in hand!
Then the cars left to applause and cheers.
Worldwide, Doddy fans wiped away tears.

Picture Them All!

Today I've given myself 3 hours' library time.
As I've got a Diddy Knotty Ash map to design!
And I've never done anything like this before.
So it's going to be a challenge, that's for sure!

I found an old map from a Knotty Ash website.
And now I will do my very best to get this right!
I have 26 places of interest on the map to plot.
As I look at the clock, just two hours left I've got!

And from those 26 places that are on my list.
In the real world, *only* four of them actually exist!
But use your imagination… open up your mind.
And those other 22 places, you will easily find!

From Doddy Towers to Knotty Ash Town Hall.
Just look on the map and then picture them all!
Anything is possible if your imagination you use.
Picture Knotty Ash harbour… its glorious views!

From Dicky Mint Lane to the Knotty Ash beach.
Everything in your imagination can be in reach!
But without a number, the landing site of a UFO.
As that's a top secret, only the Diddymen know!

The Knotty Ash 'Doddy Day' Parade

Today to Knotty Ash I've come.
To hear the sound of its drum.
So down every road and street.
I go to hear the Great Drum beat.

It's 'Doddy Day' the reason why.
As the Diddymen, all pass me by.
Doddy's big fans are all out in force.
Colin, Jan and Stephen of course!

Leaving the Happiness Train, I see.
Lots more Doddy fans on platform 3.
Irene, Rosemarie and Helen too.
And a full 10B Doddy Bus is also due.

From California, Pamela has flown.
To be in Knotty Ash, Doddy's home.
From Thomas Lane to Little Bongs.
The drum is part of Doddy songs

The Great Drum is on show today.
And other Doddy items are on display.
The street parties, started at noon.
As we sing a certain *Happiness* tune!

Ola Ness and his Red Rose Band.
Lead the parade in this magical land.
A special day in this part of the world.
As a 'Miss you Doddy' flag is unfurled.

Cont.

Passing the Chuckle Muscle Gym.
Waving tickling sticks, fans join in.
Big crowds all line Dicky Mint Lane.
Outside Doddy Towers it's the same!

It's a day of fun, this Doddy Parade.
Lots of jam butties, specially made!
Schools are closed, shops too at one.
In this land, where *our* king is from.

The King of Comedy, one of our own.
The one and only, a hero home-grown.
The Master of Mirth, much loved by all.
The parade now passes Happiness Hall.

So come along, Missus, it's not too late.
Join us in Springfield Park for our fete!
Today is 'Doddy Day'... so join in the fun.
To find us, follow the beat of the drum!

A Place To Go

In Knotty Ash, not far from Doddy's home.
A place to go, if you're feeling sad and alone.
Doddy fans meet up and talk things through.
Turn sadness into happiness they try to do.
I went there once, as I was having a sad day.
I felt unsure and nervous at what to say.
Those Doddy fans put their arms around me.
Better times ahead, they convinced me to see.
I was treated to jam butties from the mine.
And the Doddy fans cheered me up in no time.
Talking about Doddy, put a smile on my face.
I soon felt happiness return as I left that place.
So don't hide away if you're feeling a little low.
Help is out there, with other such places to go.

Knotty Ash DNA

There must be something in our DNA.
Why Knotty Ash people are this way.
Always happy, no scowl or frown.
Something our Doddy handed down!

What an example the Squire did set.
Look on the bright side, never to fret!
'Happiness' is everything he would say.
Something we take on board every day.

That's why people travel from afar.
To see just how happy, we really are!
So, if you're not convinced, visit us too.
On leaving you'll say, 'Well that was true.'

The Hair!

Have you got a few minutes to spare?
While we study Doddy's amazing hair!
Doddy's very own Diddy mountain peak.
Dicky Mint scaled it...it took him a week!

At other times, Doddy's hair looks to me.
Like television ariels, receiving the BBC!
Many years later, punks copied his style.
But Doddy's was bigger by the odd mile!

Into every direction, Doddy's hair fired.
Like into a current, it had been wired!
Hair to defy gravity, that's hard to do.
So Doddy used a magic Knotty Ash glue!

Doddy used his hair as a prop...as a tool.
To make people laugh, by acting the fool!
So his hair became famous in its own right.
Making his fans chuckle deep into the night!

What A Beautiful Day!
(The Ken Dodd Museum)

Sometime in the future, how fitting it would be.
To have a Doddy Museum for all his fans to see!
And in this museum would be a moggy skin coat.
And we all know why there should be a milk float!

And for all the millions of records Ken Dodd sold.
There would be discs of platinum, silver and gold.
Tickling sticks would be on display everywhere.
With pictures of Doddy, complete with crazy hair!

And from Knotty Ash of course, the Great Drum.
A museum bristling with such happiness and fun!
To see some stage clothes again would be a treat.
And the visitors could be given jam butties to eat!

Diddymen mementoes... books, games and toys.
And in the background, we'd hear laughter noise!
Lots more lovely Doddy items could go on display.
Above the museum it reads... 'What A Beautiful day'.

Journey

Twelve months ago, his new journey begun.
A journey beyond the stars, moon and sun.
Beyond the rainbows at his journey's end.
Welcoming him, his every absent friend.

Now he'll shine on forever in Heaven's light.
Making Angels laugh deep into the night!
Every day we miss him, we speak his name.
I always think of him as I pass Thomas Lane.

The Squire has left us, an era over for sure.
But Knotty Ash will be famous for evermore!
The entertainment world forever in your debt.
The Liverpool legend, we will never, ever forget.

Knotty Ash Town Hall

Knotty Ash has its very own Town Hall
With its own mayor, who is very small!
Around his neck is a Diddy gold chain.
He goes to work on the Happiness Train.

As mayor, he has important roles to do.
Opening treacle wells, is one of a few!
And often you'll see him, time to time.
At the grand launch of a Jam Butty Mine.

Looking all regal in his moggy skin cape.
He uses Diddy scissors to cut the tape.
Dicky Mint is the mayor's right-hand man.
Together, the best for Knotty Ash they plan.

Approval for a Doddy Museum they gave.
As the legend of our Doddy is vital to save!
Above their office, the Knotty Ash flag flies.
It shows two tickling sticks... hardly a surprise!

A Knotty Ash Bedtime Tale

A child's bedtime story, a little tale.
The children will love it, without fail.
About a fantasy land in Liverpool 14.
The most magical land ever seen!

A land where people are very small.
Nobody ever grows over three foot tall.
And funny shoes and hats they wear.
And their happy songs, fill the air!

The people there have a funny name.
A land with a very big Happiness Train.
A magical land, just one square mile.
And everyone wears a big happy smile!

Where Diddymen have their jobs to do.
In factories and mines, just to name two!
But only is jam, found down those mines.
And only biscuits on the factory lines!

Sticky treacle from the wells is free.
Broken biscuits fixed in time for your tea.
The gravy trains, they run on the hour.
The only rainfall is from a sun shower!

Cont.

In this lovely land, a happy king is sat.
He wears no crown, *just* a jester's hat!
A humble king, in no need of a throne.
As The King of Comedy, he is known!

His sticky-up hair to the sky does poke.
Wherever he goes, he tells joke after joke
A Happiness Land, full of joy and delight.
Share this tale, with your children tonight!

A Whispered Goodnight

In Knotty Ash, I once drove through.
It was very late; it was gone half past two.
On Thomas Lane, pulled up a car.
Two silhouettes shone, 'neath an L14 star.

Through darkness, I made out this pair.
It was Doddy with a tower of crazy hair!
In his arms, he carried somebody small.
I slowed down my car, to just a crawl.

And through my window, now unwound.
I heard a cute little Diddy snoring sound.
It came from Dicky Mint, eyes closed tight.
A carry to bed, and a whispered 'Goodnight.'

A Knotty Ash Tea Party.

There is a party in Knotty Ash today.
Lots of children making their way.
Dicky Mint will be the party host.
Dicky, the one, a child loves the most!
It's a Knotty Ash party, easy to tell.
With its treacle pudding from the well.
The jam served, the best you can buy.
Mined today, for party butty or pie!
Party games with a Knotty Ash theme.
Diddymen shows on the big screen.
Sounds of laughter will ring out loud.
As Doddy looks down, he'll be so proud!

The Heavenly Tour Opening Night

Well did you see last night's rain pour?
All because of Doddy's Heavenly Tour!
Floods of rain and hail in Knotty Ash fell.
So much they filled up the treacle well!

Snuff quarries under water, ankle deep.
Soggy Knotty Ash snuff, selling cheap!
Jam butties from the mine, soaking wet.
Watered-down gravy from the train, I bet!

But we Doddy fans don't mind, not at all.
Because we know, that wasn't rain to fall.
It was pools of tears from laughter shed.
As Doddy's Happiness Show went ahead.

So today, if a puddle on the road you see.
It's there down to our Doddy, I guarantee!
As passing away is not the end you know.
On another brighter journey, we simply go.

Diddy Doddy's Liverpool Weekend

Diddy Doddy's home, complete with tan!
Now my turn as host, good times to plan.
He's been on his holidays across the sea.
Now time to spend with big Doddy fan me!

But something different from me this time.
His story not in pictures, it comes in rhyme.
So read my words; please be my guest.
And let your imagination simply do the rest!

I took Diddy Doddy to St Georges Hall.
Where we saw the Giants amazingly tall,
To a Diddy Doddy they were even bigger still!
Young and old, the Giants all set to thrill!

We saw an Arriva bus that was split in 2!
Amazing the damage, a Giant's knife can do!
By the 'bombed out church' we wondered why.
A giant 2 pronged fork reached the sky!

Cont.

To the beautiful Central Library next to see.
A building Ken Dodd loved, just like me!
I took Diddy up to the roof top for the view.
I held Diddy tightly as the high wind blew!

Match day arrived, Manchester City in Town!
Liverpool so desperate to regain their crown!
I christened Diddy Doddy a 'Kopite' that day.
Before we watched those famous Reds play.

We saw in the Museum our Liverpool past.
Our heritage, Lennon and a famous scouse cast.
Diddy Doddy and I stood beneath the '3 graces'.
As the Liver birds peered with watchful faces.

Another verse to add to our Liverpool tale.
Across the River Mersey we both set sail.
Not quite the Mediterranean or an ocean blue.
But *nothing* can rival *our* Waterfront view!

Next thing to do with Diddy on my 'to do' list.
Was to visit the land where Diddymen exist.
In my beloved Knotty Ash, we spent some time.
And together we discovered a Jam Butty Mine!

Not much mileage over our weekend to clock.
No airports, no passports, no ships to dock!
Because what I decided while I was Diddy's host.
Was to spend 3 days in the City that we *love* most!

The reference to all things 'Giant' are to do with a set of giant marionettes, built by French theatre company Royal de Luxe who have visited Liverpool on several occasions. During the night, the Giants would often get up to mischief, hence the lines about the Arriva Bus being split in two with a Giant knife!

The 'Doddy Arms' Bar

If you fancy a drink and time to unwind.
There are lovely pubs in Knotty Ash to find.
The Doddy Arms is the favourite of mine.
The only place they sell Knotty Ash wine!

A vintage wine, every year, white or red.
Made from grapes that Diddymen tread!
The finest pub for the best beers too.
Served with snacks or Knotty Ash stew!

And this pub naturally has a Doddy theme.
Classic Doddy shown on the TV screen.
Lovers of Ken's music are also catered for.
With a juke box full of his hits and more!

Bring the little ones, lots of fun for them.
They can have a laugh with the Diddymen!
If you're a dog owner, don't leave it at home.
Ken's express wish, don't leave them alone!

With a warm Knotty Ash welcome at the door.
The Doddy Arms... you couldn't ask for more.
Join all the happy customers from near and far.
In the countries friendliest and happiest bar!

The Master Laughter Maker

The King of Knotty Ash, The Squire, The Mayor.
Laughter followed Doddy around everywhere!
The hair tousled and teased, a pull of the face.
Chuckle muscles everywhere pulled out of place!
Happiness, he spread, on every journey made.
An audience in hysterics, in every theatre played.
The Guvnor, The Jester, The Record Breaker.
The indisputable all-time master laughter maker!
From Liverpool too, so proud he's one of our own.
Ken Dodd… a legend, beyond his Knotty Ash home.

Best Place Ever!

In Knotty Ash, it's a busy old time.
As Diddymen work down the mine.
Mining for jam for your butties or jar.
Knotty Ash jam, the very best by far!

It's a busy time in Knotty Ash today.
As factory workers, make their way.
On assembly lines, biscuits to repair.
As happy Diddymen songs fill the air!

Plantation black puddings taste great.
So put them on your breakfast plate!
In Knotty Ash, lovely treacle we sell.
Freshly served from our very own well.

Of our gravy trains, please take note.
Should you need gravy for your boat!
What a place to live, to work and be.
The best place ever, Knotty Ash for me

Dicky Mint Lane

A new road in Knotty Ash, now given a name.
From today it's to be called Dicky Mint Lane.
A well-deserved tribute to Doddy's best mate.
On it to be opened a Diddy housing estate!
Diddy houses, Diddy gardens, and Diddy rent!
For only Diddy people, this estate is meant.
Every house has its own Diddy parking place.
In the centre of the estate, a big green space.
That is the place you can find something tall.
A huge statue of Doddy, to be seen by all!
It's next to a red pillar box, to post Diddy mail.
Very soon all these houses will be up for sale!
All in tickling stick colours, red, white and blue.
Only wish I was Diddy, so I could live there too!

Reading Time In Knotty Ash

Dicky Mint sat at home on the first night of spring.
Watching old clips on TV, when Doddy was king!
An evening of Doddy TV over, now it's time to read.
Dicky was missing his best mate; Doddy he did need!

Dicky turned off the television, dark was the screen.
He got together his pals, the entire Diddyman team.
It was reading time for the Diddymen, eagerly they sat.
Absent Friends the title, what better book than that?

Dicky moved the bookmark from the last page he read.
He noticed a little stain from a tear he must have shed.
Dicky composed himself, from the book he read aloud.
And with every single word, Dicky Mint felt so proud!

The Diddymen sat in silence, listening to every word.
The stories and poetry were the best they'd ever heard.
And punctuating the silence, Diddy giggles filled the air.
As they laughed at funny tales, Doddy fans had to share!

Soon Dicky put down the book, time was getting late.
For more Doddy tributes, his 'audience' would have to wait.
Dicky Mint closed the book, and said 'Goodnight' to all.
He saw another stained page, where another tear did fall.

The Perfect Gel!

Eric and Ernie, Cannon and Ball.
Stan and Ollie, I loved them all!
Mike and Bernie, laughs to share.
Chuckle Brothers, a funny pair!

Double act, Lord Charles and Ray.
Made me laugh, back in the day.
French and Saunders, funny too.
Ant and Dec, the best of the new!

The Two Ronnies, a duo supreme.
Ade and Rik, I loved that team!
Bill and Ben, The Flowerpot Men.
Love them now and loved them then!

But Dicky and Doddy, top the lot.
Double the laughs we always got.
Laugh upon laugh, night after night.
When these two shared the spotlight!

Mischievous Dicky Mint, for sure.
Winding our poor Doddy up galore!
But always done with a glint in his eye.
He loved Doddy, nobody can deny!

On the road together, tour on tour.
Getting home to Knotty Ash at 3 or 4!
They loved each other, clear to tell.
Doddy and Dicky Mint, the perfect gel!

Our Absent Friend This Christmas

In Knotty Ash the Christmas bells ring.
Carols inside church halls, people sing.
Sing just one of those carols if you will.
For our Doddy, who his fans miss still.

In Knotty Ash the snow begins to fall.
Children make snowmen, Diddymen tall.
And just a minute of your time it'll take.
To think of Doddy when you see a flake.

In Knotty Ash, Santa will be on his sleigh.
Landing on Doddy's house, a visit to pay.
Presents to deliver to Dicky Mint and co.
Alas none for Doddy, in Heaven we know.

In Knotty Ash, Christmas lights do shine.
It's a joyous occasion as it's party time!
During your party, stop to make a toast.
To the legend, Doddy, Knotty Ash can boast!

And to all you many Doddy fans out there.
This poem and message with you I share.
Have a lovely Christmas, 'happiness' no end.
Though sadly we still miss our absent friend.

Knotty Ash Barber Shop

On East Prescott Road, a barber is there.
The place to go if you want Doddy-style hair.
He can make your hair stand up on end.
On leaving the shop door, you have to bend!

To get that style he uses a special Diddy gel.
Only in Knotty Ash such a product they sell!
Like lots of things in Knotty Ash, it is unique.
It can transform your hair into a mountain peak!

To some people it may be a style too extreme.
But everybody had it in my Knotty Ash dream!
To all you older gents, a little bit of kind advice.
It's a hair product only... so please think twice!

White Feather

There are no tickling sticks to be seen.
An empty stage, but spotlights beam.
Sadly, no Knotty Ash drum in sight.
No laughter from the Grand tonight.

And no beautiful songs for us to hear.
No ventriloquist act... 'gottle of geer'!
The funniest man ever is not in town.
The final curtain has now come down.

No funny faces, no moggy skin coat.
No going home on an early milk float!
No full house to embrace and engage.
But a white feather now I see on stage.

Beautiful, poignant Photo by Gladys Chucklebutty

The Diddymen Christmas Message, 2022

In Knotty Ash it's got great appeal.
The Diddymen's Christmas meal!
Starters, treacle soup from the well.
What comes next... it's easy to tell!

It's festive jam butties for the main
Next come biccies, chocky or plain.
Biscuits fixed from the factory floor.
For drinks a 'gottle of geer' to pour!

And when all their tummies are full.
In Doddy's name a cracker they pull!
In front of Diddy flame of a Diddy fire.
They make their toast to The Squire.

'Happy Christmas' the Diddymen say.
'We miss you Doddy, every single day'
And finally, a message from me to you.
'Have a very Merry Christmas... 2022.'

Just a Mic Stand!

He put most other comedians in the shade.
To make people laugh, he was tailor-made!
With built-in props, with *such* teeth and hair!
He had such a head start; it didn't seem fair!

Of course, Doddy did use other props too.
Those tickling sticks stuck to Doddy like glue!
And I loved his 'Great Drum of Knotty Ash'
Fingers in my ears as Ken gave it the big bash!

But to call Dicky Mint a 'prop' would be a slur.
On stage he and Doddy made the perfect pair!
But put Doddy on stage with *just* a mic stand.
He'd still be the funniest comedian in the land!

Back In Knotty Ash (I'd Rather Be)

From your loaf, get 2 slices of bread.
Put on some butter...evenly spread.
Put away the cheese, bacon or ham.
For this butty, you *only* require Jam!
When I was a Diddy Knotty Ash lad.
They were the best butties I ever had.
Strawberry Jam, Raspberry or Plum.
They all tasted lovely, made by Mum!
Eating one now, I've gone back in time.
To when I lived by a Jam Butty Mine!
I'm older now, travelled land and sea.
But back in Knotty Ash, I'd rather be.
Now, as I write this, with butty in hand.
It takes me back to that Magical Land!

The Sir Ken Dodd Happiness Hall, 25 September 2021
The Liverpool Theatre Event

I jump out of my bed, it's an exciting day!
To the Happiness Hall, I'll make my way.
But first my brekkie, a Diddy jam butty roll.
Then I pour my Doddy Flakes into my bowl.
Off to the bus stop, the Doddy 10B is due.
So, I join the other children in the queue.
Then off to nearby Thomas Lane we all go.
To Doddy's old school, wouldn't you know!
A theatre master class is taking place there.
I can't wait to see what advice it will share.
To develop budding young performers its aim.
And it all takes place under Doddy's name!
It's for ages five to sixteen and the sessions are free.
Doddy would love this... same goes for me!

At Home

In the Central Library, Doddy felt at home.
In a Shakespeare play, another comfort zone!
A massive or a small audience to please.
Doddy could do either with a confident ease!

In front of the TV cameras, for a live show.
Our Doddy was the master, the ultimate pro.
In documentaries, he was never out of place.
At home whenever serious issues to face.

An event to open, a speech as invited guest.
Doddy was a natural, and passed every test!
As Doddy just being Doddy, would get him by.
A clever, natural, funny man, the reason why!

'Tickle Tonic'

With that hairstyle, teased into a peak.
And his trademark teeth, an image unique!
Doddy made you laugh with looks alone.
Humour then rammed the laughter home!

Be it lengthy stories or a classic one-liner.
As comedians go, there was nobody finer!
For catchphrases too, Ken was renowned.
A language of his own, Doddy had found!

Words not found in the dictionary for sure.
A Doddy edition needed in every bookstore!
A 'tickle tonic' was Doddy, take as required!
Laugh yourself better from every joke fired!

'Doddyween', 31 October 2022

In Knotty Ash, it's time for 'Doddyween'.
All Hallows Eve, but with a Doddy theme!
Doddy masks and wigs, wear the local folk.
And for their treat, get told a Doddy joke!

All households also give out an extra treat.
A goody bag filled with jam butties to eat!
It's a night of happiness on the 31st.
Nothing spooky, nothing scary or cursed!

No witches in sight, not a sign of ghouls.
In Knotty Ash, we have our *own* set of rules!
As everything we do is happiness based!
Any chance to have of fun, we never waste!

Chuckle muscles are kept active this way.
They barely get a rest, come night or day!
So, any howling you may hear on this night.
Will just be howls of laughter... *not* of fright!

'Doddy Airlines'

Knotty Ash Airport is so friendly and green.
It's the Diddiest Airport there's ever been.
They fly just tiny planes to magical places.
A plane full of happy, Knotty Ash faces!

Dicky Mint is the pilot of 'Doddy Airlines'
It's his second job, when not in the mines!
He loves taking off into the Knotty Ash sky.
It creates such happiness, the reason why!

Jet fuel replaced by a cleaner power source.
As the sound of laughter is *more* of a force!
On the ground with tickling sticks in hand.
Dicky's plane, is waved safely down to land!

The Knotty Ash Jam Shortage, 3 January 2023

It's back to work, now it's the 3rd of Jan.
As in Knotty Ash, there's a shortage of Jam!
So many jam butties have been consumed.
Now work in the mines, today is resumed!
Treacle levels in shops are dangerously low.
So today to the wells, the Diddymen will go!
And there's thousands of biscuits to repair.
Dropped and broken over the festive fayre.
'And there's a lack a gravy,' I hear you cry!
The shops in Knotty Ash, have now run dry.
The gravy in Knotty Ash, people love most.
Has been all used up on the festive roast!
But the gravy trains, will bring it all back.
As the Diddymen return to the railway track
Of moggy skin coats, we have sold the lot.
So back to the Ranch today, for Harry Cott!
But, all these jobs are Diddy, a 30-minute chore.
That's why such a job, I've been looking for!

Haha…. Since the previous poems about Doddy in goal, he went on to better things, not by being any good, but by doing what he's best at… making people laugh and missing their target!!

The Cup Final Penalty Shoot-Out
(with Doddy in Goal!)

It's a cup final penalty shoot-out.
Liverpool are in with a great shout!
As our Doddy's between the sticks.
And he's up to some funny tricks!

As the penalty-taker starts his run.
Doddy decides to have some fun!
He starts playing about with his hair.
He gives the player a funny stare.

Part of the ploy, hair, teeth and eyes.
Then over the bar the penalty flies!
That ball is actually Jupiter bound.
And from The Kop, a laughing sound!

And on it went, each pen the same.
Doddy's hilarious antics to blame!
So Liverpool won on pens, 3-0.
But the *losing* side are laughing still!

The Sir Ken Dodd Happiness Hall
(Doddy Fan's Get Together 29/7/23)

On the 29th July, come to Happiness Hall.
Tell all your Doddy pals, give them a call!
Great Doddy memories we can all share
Lady Dodd and John Martin will be there!

Two great female singers performing too.
Don't miss this event, fans old and new!
Come along Missus, bring your 'old man'
We have a *Diddy* buffet...butties with jam!

Also on the menu, a Plumptious Hot Pot.
By Jove, Vera's event has got the lot!
Broken biscuit's too, served from a tin.
Plus, a Diddy Raffle...great prizes to win!

I'll also have my new Doddy book to sell.
Proceeds from it, to a good cause as well!
It'll be a magical night, full of fun and song.
So, to Happiness Hall, *please* come along!

CHAPTER 7

The Happiness Train Series of Poetry (11–20)

Continuing where we left off in Chapter 1, with the delay in the Happiness Train leaving Rhyl, we now have a replacement driver to take the train to Knotty Ash... Unfortunately, things didn't get much better!!

All aboard and read on!

Happiness Train 11 (Replacement Driver Surprise!)

Well would you believe it... lo and behold?
Guess what information we've been told?
The new driver is for your Happiness Train.
The one and only... Dicky Mint his name!

He's a very funny Diddyman, as we all know.
Dicky and Doddy the perfect two-man show!
So Dicky has driven off, on the Doddy Line.
We're hoping he gets to Knotty Ash on time!

Cont.

The train blew puffs of happiness smoke.
Dicky Mint was telling many a Doddy joke!
The crew were all laughing, as it pulled away.
Somehow, we're expecting a further delay!

A laugh-filled atmosphere, Dicky had created.
Sorry, all we can do is to keep you updated!
But the odds of the train being on time are small!
But it is called 'the Happiness Train', after all!

'For all you Doddy fans, Irene, Vera and Jan.
'Sorry, but there's been another change of plan!
'On route, Dicky Mint got lost along the way.
'Asking for directions "Knotty Ash" he couldn't say!'

So, Dicky went to Blackpool North instead.
The Happiness Train he drove, full steam ahead!
So, it didn't take long, with all that Diddy power.
To arrive in lovely Blackpool, just by the Tower!

Dicky Mint had a plan, so he went to the Grand.
And asked his mate Shaun Gorringe for a hand!
'Any chance you can come to Liverpool with me?
I'm on the way to Knotty Ash and got lost, you see!'

Shaun and Dicky Mint go back an awful long way.
Shaun was eager to help, and prevent further delay.
They left on the Happiness Train in a bit of a dash.
To finally pick those Doddy fans from Knotty Ash!

Back in Knotty Ash, the fans waited in Happiness Hall.
They shared Doddy tales and we're having a ball!
They helped themselves to a Diddy jam butty spread.
As the Happiness Train and Dicky to Knotty Ash sped.

Happiness Train 12 (Lock Down Wish!)

When lockdown is over, whenever that may be.
Do you want to share a special journey with me?
A journey where mates can meet up once more.
To share laughs and memories of Doddy galore!

Exercise our chuckle muscles, no need of a gym.
These muscles are special, and need to be trim!
So, on the Happiness Train, that's what we'll do.
A journey of howling fun, please come along too.

When lockdown is over, it'll be just what we need.
When from all the restrictions, we're finally freed!
The Happiness Train will be waiting, raring to go.
It will be next best thing to an actual Doddy show!

The next Happiness Train journey, please be soon.
Imagine how far it will go to replace all the gloom!
To put these troubled times behind us, I can't wait.
Then on the Happiness Train, we can all celebrate!

Happiness Train 13 (Ladies Day Special!)

To all you lovely Knotty Ash ladies and beyond.
Wherever you come from, over land and pond.
Today the Happiness Train is reserved for you.
You'll have to be a 'Missus' to join this queue!

We leave Knotty Ash Station, sunshine or rain.
No fellas allowed today on the Happiness Train.
Diddy checks will be made for stowaway men!
Bring your jam butties for lunch, we leave at 10.

Have a natter and laugh, ladies, come on board.
All passengers will be here for the same accord!
No, Missus, not just to leave the old man behind!
But to share Doddy stories, as he's one of a kind.

It'll be a journey full of happy memories and fun.
No ticket is required, just a smile and you're done!
It's International Women's Day, hop on, be proud.
That's why it's ladies only today, no fellas allowed!

Happiness Train 14
(The Advert Campaign!)

For you today, another Happiness Train tale.
As you know, we don't have tickets for sale!
This train service is not run for profit or gain.
It runs to promote happiness, in Ken's name.

This Doddy fans' train runs across the nation.
It picks up anywhere, just name your station!
Trains run every day, a very flexible timetable.
So, Doddy fans come aboard, if you are able.

We serve hot and cold food on every train ride.
A special Knotty Ash menu, we always provide.
But very sorry, Missus, it's nothing too grand!
But it includes the best jam butties in the land!

It's a dog-friendly train, so please bring your pet.
Lots of factory broken biscuits, they will get!
Lady Dodd and Dicky Mint often come along too.
They share their Doddy tales, just like we all do!

Extra wide seats to stretch your new knee or hip.
Zimmer frames available, to prevent fall or a trip!
If you're a first-time traveller, please don't be shy.
Doddy fans are a friendly bunch, the reason why!

Cont.

On this special train, every day is a beautiful day.
Just ask big Doddy fan Pamela, from the USA!
Other lovely fans aboard, you might get to know.
Rosemarie, Colin France, Stephen, young comic Joe!

And there are the regular travellers, Irene and Jan.
Vera, Jade, Mary, and fab artists Allan and Sam!
Please Doddy fans, join us on the Happiness Train.
That's the Diddy message of our Advert campaign!

No offence intended with my reference to hip and knee replacements (I am waiting for a total knee replacement myself!). Just a gentle bit of fun regarding Doddy's ageing (and of course loyal!) audience during his latter year shows. Doddy himself often quipped about it. In Southport, Doddy once said, 'By Jove, looking at you lot, the Southport care homes must be empty tonight!'

Happiness Train 15 (Bank Holiday Special!)

The second bank holiday of the month today.
These means summertime is on the way!
If you're leaving Knotty Ash to go anywhere.
The Happiness Train will take you there.

No tickets of course needed for your trips.
Just show a big happy smile across your lips!
Smiling and happiness our currency of choice.
And also bring along your singing voice.

As lots of happy songs we sing, once aboard.
Please arrive early, so your place is secured.
The Happiness Train is always full for sure.
The Bank Holiday Special goes from platform 4.

On board there is a Knotty Ash souvenir shop.
But don't get caught out and miss your stop!
As it happens all the time, every journey we run.
People forget to get off as having too much fun!

The Happiness Train 16
(Post-Lockdown to Blackpool Trip!)

Lockdown is over... let's all celebrate!
The Happiness Train will leave at 8.
A trip to Blackpool we have planned.
All talk of Covid onboard is banned!

Instead let's talk about Doddy all day.
And we'll eat jam butties on the way.
Fresh from the mine, prepared by me.
Dicky Mint helped, over a cup of tea.

At 8am we leave Knotty Ash, platform 1.
Please come along, wherever you're from.
No ticket is needed, that's not our style.
To board, just produce a big happy smile!

Happiness Train 17
(Freedom Day, 19 July 2021!)

Finally, after a month's further delay.
July 19th is here, our 'Freedom Day'!
So back on track and restriction free.
The happiest train you will ever see!

As we Doddy fans make it that way.
So, join us all on board... no fare to pay.
Just replace your mask with a smile.
Let's hug each other, it's been a while!

We've made no plans on where to go.
It'll be great fun that much we know!
'Hands in the bucket' or a 'Diddy Dip'.
That's how well decide this latest trip!

We might stay local, or Euston maybe!
Or Blackpool North, a day by the sea!
We'll share Doddy tales, pics and more.
A joyous Freedom Day... that's for sure!

Into our famous jam butties, we'll tuck.
Dicky Mint might join us, if we're in luck!
So, at Knotty Ash Station, please be there.
The golden rule being, a smile is your fare!

And that golden rule will always apply.
This is the Happiness Train, that is why!
A unique train for all Doddy fans to meet.
'Happiness always', until each trip complete!

The Happiness Train 18
(Chuckle Muscle Special)

I'm just getting ready in Doddy Towers.
The Happiness Train leaves in three hours.
And if you want, I'll reserve you a seat.
Then later today in Lime St, we'll meet.

If you feel a bit down, post festive blues.
Don't worry, Missus, our aim is to amuse!
By Jove, we'll amuse, please be assured.
So please come along and jump on board!

Leave all your troubles and cares behind.
There's no better way to relax and unwind!
The perfect pick-me-up that's our aim.
That's what you get on the Happiness Train!

Laughter will fill each compartment and aisle.
Your happiness will return, with every mile!
So, if your chuckle muscles are on the wane.
We'll put that right, on the Happiness Train!

Happiness Train 19...
Christmas Wishes 2022

It's the year 2022, it's Christmas time.
Guess what's leaving from platform 9?
It's left from there many times before.
To the tune of joy and happiness galore.

I'm sure by now that you know its name.
So, no more of this little guessing game!
It's the Happiness Train, about to go.
Full of Doddy fans, who you may know.

And I'm sure by now you are all aware.
That a big smile is your ticket... your fare!
No money on this train changes hands.
Today we're off to the Blackpool sands.

So have a smile ready, say 'Cheese' and grin.
As your *happy* journey is about to begin.
A trip shared by Doddy fans old and new.
My Christmas wishes to every one of you!

The Happiness Train 20
(The Royalty Special)

Hurry up, Missus and get out of the rain.
And jump on board the Happiness Train.
Tickets, not needed, no cash nor cheque.
Just produce a big smile and find a spec!

You're just in time, as we are running late.
As for Dicky Mint, we are having to wait.
I think Dicky forgot; he is our driver today.
So, while we wait, Doddy songs we play!

Today, we can welcome royalty on board.
As Doddy 'knighted' them, not with sword!
A tickling stick tap, a princess they became.
Amie, Emma, Lucy, each princess by name!

That story is really true; they will tell you so.
Now, always recognised, wherever they go!
Our distinguished guests will share their tale.
On the Happiness Train today, on Merseyrail!

CHAPTER 8

Doddy Back on The Box!

As I was coming to the end of working on this book, it was announced, to the great delight of Doddy's legion of loyal followers, that there was to be a new tribute TV programme dedicated to the Master of Mirth.

The programme was to be called 'Ken Dodd: 30 Funniest Moments' and was to be screened on Channel 5 on 13 August 2022. This one-off, two-hour documentary was welcomed with great anticipation by fans of Sir Ken Dodd... and it didn't disappoint!

The programme was fantastic viewing, with lovely and sincere tributes coming from a whole host of Doddy's close friends and fellow pros, and there were of course lots of memorable Doddy footage with him in many of his guises.

I wrote two poems before the show was broadcast and three afterwards, so I thought I would include them in a Diddy chapter all of their own to close this book.

The 'Giggle Map' poem is included among this set of poems because it was something I had forgotten all about until Doddy briefly mentioned it on the show, so it then became the subject of a new poem!

Back on the Box!

Doddy is back... back on the box!
Set your timers, set your clocks!
This is a show not to be missed.
Add it to your 'must-watch' list!

Claim the telly from the old man.
Unless of course he's also a fan!
Make a cup of tea, and jam butty.
Cancel all calls... ignore the footy!

This is a programme long overdue.
So don't miss it, whatever you do!
Doddy on Saturday, prime time TV.
In front of your telly, the place to be!

Any plans you have, let them wait.
The TV show of the year starts at 8!
Chuckle muscles, all pulled for sure.
Be aware viewers... there is no cure!

KEN DODD

30 FUNNIEST MOMENTS

Comedy Gold

Calling all you TV viewers tonight.
On the way, two hours of pure delight.
Must-watch telly, second to none.
Enjoy a one-off legend, the only one!
Dazzling Doddy, you just can't beat!
Your chuckle muscles, in for a treat.

Glorious Doddy, playing many a part.
Only thirty best moments, where to start?
Lots won't be shown, thousands I'd say.
Doddy was the greatest, in every way!

Ken Dodd: 30 Funniest Moments

TV documentary ∘ Channel 5 ∘ 2022 ∘ 1 episode

A two-hour documentary looking at the work of Ken Dodd. Also features Anita Harris, Roger McGough, Ricky Tomlinson and David Morrissey.

Due to be broadcast on Saturday 13th August on C5 at 8pm

Doddy to a T!

Sir Ken Dodd... a lifelong hero of mine
Now a new TV show... not before time!
So much fantastic material in the can.
A long follow-up series, they should plan!

But this show was a great place to start.
It showed Doddy treat comedy as an art.
We got to see our Doddy in many a role.
To spread happiness, that was his goal.

We saw some film footage, quite scarce.
Poet Roger McGough, read some verse.
We heard how funny words came to be.
I learnt some things that were new to me!

The Diddymen of course got an airing.
Doddy and Dicky Mint the perfect pairing!
Giggle maps, one-liners and falling boots.
Funny hairdos, catch phases, funny suits!

They showed Ken throughout the times.
We heard all about the Jam Butty Mines.
We saw Doddy when he became a knight.
Saw a record-breaking Doddy in full flight!

Cont.

Difficult times we saw Doddy overcome.
We saw him beating the Knotty Ash Drum!
We saw Doddy talking on a ferry boat.
And looking all funny in a moggy skin coat!

Guests included scousers, John and Claire.
Many tickling sticks we saw waved in the air!
Doddy the great actor, we saw in Dr Who.
And of course, Doddy played Malvolio too!

A whole nation glued to their television sets.
Watching the best TV show this year we'll get!
A 'one-man variety show' that's Doddy to a T.
The best all round entertainer, we'll ever see!

Doddy's 'Giggle Map'

Doddy was miles ahead of his time.
And that's the subject of this rhyme
Decades before Google Maps began.
When journeys were harder to plan.

Doddy had invented a map of his own.
The focal point, Knotty Ash, his home!
Called a 'Giggle Map' complete with key.
But this map was different, as we'll see!

Doddy's Giggle Map was of the UK.
A map of the all the places he did play.
Theatres across the nation, big or small.
Doddy's Giggle Map included them all!

Best response to gags, Ken noted down.
Because tastes differed, town to town.
Caring Doddy took all that info on board.
What went down well, what struck a chord.

Doddy was serious about his craft, his art.
He understood what set an audience apart.
And he honed his act, to his Giggle Map refer.
So, for every show, he knew how to prepare!

Wherever Ken travelled, wherever he went
Doddy would learn lessons from each event.
Then on his Giggle Map, that info would go.
So, he could give his fans the very best show!

...umentary series, Kate Williams ...am House; 4 of 8. explores the history of the royal estate in Norfolk, which was purchased in 1861 and is one of the few royal residences owned personally by the Windsors. (Rpt)

8.00 Ken Dodd: 30 Funniest Moments

New ★

One-off celebration of the comedian, who was embraced by the emerging TV age, while always keeping alive the old-school comedy of the music hall. Through his amazing routines, interview and one-liners, the programme examine the career of this student of comedy, wh was also a highly successful recording artist. With contributions by fans, frienc and colleagues from down the years, including Anita Harris, Roger McGougl Ricky Tomlinson and David Morrissey.

0 When Classic TV Goes Horribly

And so, my Doddy friends, to the final poem in my book, which is dedicated to the one and only Sir Ken Dodd. Thank you very much for reading; I hope you enjoyed it! This final poem, quite appropriately, is called 'Laughed My Socks Off!'.

Laughed My Socks Off!

Because Doddy delivers at the speed of sound.
I might have missed something first time round!
So, thank goodness for catch-up TV, I say.
As I watch Doddy's show for the third time today!
So, with the remote control firmly in my hand.
I tune in to My 5... the station for TV on demand.
What I missed before, I'll try and catch this time.
Maybe I missed a favourite Doddy joke of mine!
Because I know I've heard all of the jokes before.
But that doesn't mean, I can't hear them once more!
Of those fab jokes, my chuckle muscles never tire.
That's why he's so unique, the Knotty Ash Squire!
I could watch over and over again, his same routine.
And still laugh my socks off, be it on stage or screen.

Hold the press...Hold the press! Just as I was about to submit my manuscript to the publisher I came up with this very different type of poem (what do you mean, Missus, 'a good one?')

This poem fits the format and tune of the famous song *In My Liverpool Home*.

In My Knotty Ash Home

In my Knotty Ash home... in my Knotty Ash home.

If you stay long enough, you'll hear Diddymen songs.
We have rows of cottages, that we call Little Bongs.
If you love jam butties, we have plenty to sell.
We have our own treacle, that's fresh from the well.

In my Knotty Ash home... in my Knotty Ash home.

The funniest man ever, lived his entire life here.
And we still miss our Doddy, each day of the year!
We're born with chuckle muscles, how lucky are we!
And if you want a princess, then you'll find we have 3!

Cont.

In my Knotty Ash home... in my Knotty Ash home.

We have a Happiness Train... just smile for the fare!
We have Doddy Towers and the Comedy Square!
Dicky Mint lives here, but by no means, that's all.
We have the Moggy Ranch and a Happiness Hall.

In my Knotty Ash home... in my Knotty Ash home.

We fix broken biscuits, until they're OK to eat.
Everyday a Diddymen, you are likely, to meet.
Knotty Ash is the home of Diddy Harry Cott.
In my Knotty Ash home, everything we have got!

In my Knotty Ash home... in my Knotty Ash home.

We have the Doddy Channel; on boats we can sail.
Aliens have been here, that's our top-secret tale!
If you want a Doddy Bus, then we have the 10B.
In my Knotty Ash home, all these things you can see!

In my Knotty Ash home... in my Knotty Ash home.

Acknowledgements

The years 2021 and 2022 were extremely difficult and traumatic for me. My Mum's health was in serious decline and she was in and out of hospital on numerous occasions. Due to Covid restrictions, spending time with her was very limited during this frustrating, tearful and lonely period.

My mum sadly passed away peacefully in her sleep on 6 November 2021... typical of my mum – without a word of self-pity or complaint.

I owe a huge 'thank you' to the following family and friends who helped me through the most difficult time of my life following my mum's passing. Without their kind help and support, I doubt I could have continued work on this book.

My beautiful Daughters, Emma Bartram and Rachel Bartram.
Big brother, Stephen Bartram (aka Sam).
Little brother, Jon Bartram.
Little sister, Bernadette Bartram.
My wonderful niece, Lucinda Bartram.
My gorgeous granddaughters Alba and Nola and their Dad, Michael Shelbourne

My best friends:
Yaowaret Khamnang
Maureen Hopper
Siobhan Houston
Simona Retkova
Rooney, Saint and Princess Emily

Sirichomchan Denny
Nancy, Koko, Jeab, Tuk, Jo and Cherry

I thank you all every night and day.
For every tear, you helped wipe away.
xx

All poems by Michael Bartram written between 2018 and 2023.

Front cover photograph by Stephen Shakeshaft (greatly admired by Doddy, who referred to Stephen as 'the happy snapper')/the *Liverpool Echo*, licensed for use by Alamy (www.alamy.com).

Front/back cover designs by www.photofirstaid.co.uk. And many thanks (as ever!) to Oliver and Jen at Photofirstaid for enhancement work on images and for their kind advice and patience along the way.

Book layout/design by Michael Bartram/Grosvenor House Publishing.

Happiness Train artwork by Tomacco,

Getty Images

Doddy chuckle muscle apron and T-shirt available at www.redbubble.com.

Fantastic artwork provided by big Doddy fans Allan Taylor, Daniel Hanton and Gladys Chucklebutty. Thank you so much for your wonderful contributions – they are really appreciated!

Thanks to peterkayephotography@gmail.com.

Thanks to www.stephendavies.me.uk for image enhancement.

This publication has been self-funded and donations from all sales will go to The Children's Air Ambulance Service, registered charity www.theairambulanceservice.org.uk.

A big thank you to Vera Yorke and Colin France for the running of their wonderful and friendly Doddy Facebook groups (**Friends of Sir Ken Dodd and Sir Ken Dodd Appreciation Society**).

Thank you to the kind staff at the Breck Road Community Library for all those 'extra' hours they allocated to me while working on this book. brecklibrary@altvalley.co.uk.

Book promo bookmarks and other great graphic design work by **www.allianceprint.co.uk**

For all your **HAPPY** printing go to **info@banana-print.co.uk**

Thank you very much for reading and until next time, Tatty bye everybody, Tatty bye!

Michael Bartram
(dandy662021@outlook.com)
January 2023

Other publications by the author:

Hillsborough 20 Years On. ISBN 9781906823153

Justice Call: My Hillsborough Poems. ISBN 9781906823283.

The Nightmare of Hillsborough. ISBN 9781906828498.

25 Years of Hillsborough Pain. ISBN 9781906823979.

Hillsborough… Our Greatest Victory. ISBN 9781786238825.

Road Safety and Awareness: In Memory of Bobby Colleran. ISBN 9781786238825.

RoadPeace Poetry. ISBN 9781786232410.

Absent Friends: A Tribute to Sir Ken Dodd. ISBN 9781786233233.

Ingram Content Group UK Ltd.
Milton Keynes UK
UKHW021016220623
423823UK00010B/116